Pride and Produce

The origin, evolution, and survival of the Drowned Lands, the Hudson Valley's legendary Black Dirt farming region

D1522154

Kudos to Cheetah Haysom for *Pride and Produce* an engaging, informative and penetrating story of a well-known but poorly understood food producing region of North America. These so-called Drowned Lands hold the largest accumulation of the richest soil in our nation. One and a quarter the size of Manhattan island with over 26,000 acres it boasts of some of the most fertile farmland in North America. It also offers a compelling history of human and natural diversity in a Garden of Eden.

Haysom takes us on a fascinating journey into the mysterious Drowned Lands from the prehistoric era to today, from the Ice Age and early Native Americans to the Age of Global Warming. With uncanny insight we are introduced to its organically-rich black dirt, its hydrology, its flora and fauna, its bountiful crops and the proud but dirt poor immigrants from eastern Europe who within two generations transformed this tangled wetland into one of America's most productive agricultural food sheds, feeding millions of metropolitan consumers while achieving prosperity and a good life for their families. Agricultural empires were made and unmade in an environment of extended-family dynastic rivalries and marital attachments. Haysom dispassionately captures the fascinating dynamics of this. We see interesting personalities emerging in the book and the responses of surrounding communities to their trials and tribulations. This is indeed an intensely human story of struggles among themselves, of perseverance in the face natural and man-made disasters, of navigating labyrinthine government bureaucracies. It is a saga of struggle for sustainability and survival against all odds. Setting her story in historical perspective Haysom ponders these challenges and contemplates the future of black dirt farming.

In this provocative and important study we discover that the problems facing these indomitable yet vulnerable Hudson River valley farming families are problems that are nationwide and with national consequences. This book is an urgent and alarming wake-up call for Americans to better appreciate and understand where their food comes from, how is it produced, who produces and markets it and its culinary and nutritional value. If you don't know much about onions, for example, you will from Haysom's vivid and enticing explorations into a region once known as the onion capital of America..

After years of exhaustive research including interviews with the farmers and migrant field hands Haysom has woven an amazing tapestry of the trials and tribulations of modern farming. She gives life and meaning to her informants and makes the reader feel they too are participants in the unfolding drama. Haysom brings refreshing clarity to the complex issues of preserving a nationally-important and ecologically rich freshwater wetland while ensuring the commercial food producing viability of what is becoming the most important food-producing region in the tri-state New York region. The unfolding struggle in America between advocates of wetland preservation and reclamation and the imperatives of food production is brought into sharp focus through this an intensive examination at the local grassroots level.

Cheetah Haysom, a prominent and seasoned journalist who lives in the Black Dirt community of Pine Island has crafted an immensely readable and timely book. It is a must-read for anyone interested in environmental and community history, migrants and ethnicity, social and cultural diversity, food, farming and labor relations.

Dr. Richard Hull
Professor Emeritus of History
New York University
Municipal Historian, Town of Warwick, New York

Pride and Produce

THE ORIGIN, EVOLUTION, AND SURVIVAL OF THE DROWNED LANDS,
THE HUDSON VALLEY'S LEGENDARY BLACK DIRT FARMING REGION

Cheetah Haysom

Drowned Lands Press
New York, NY

Printed in the United States of America

Third Printing, 2019 *Updated Edition*

ISBN 978-1-54399-628-9

Drowned Lands Press
10 Mitchell Place
New York, NY 10017
e-mail: cheetah@daparma.us.com

Cover photo: Bob Breese/breesepix.com
Cover & book design layout: Peter Lyons Hall

TABLE OF CONTENTS

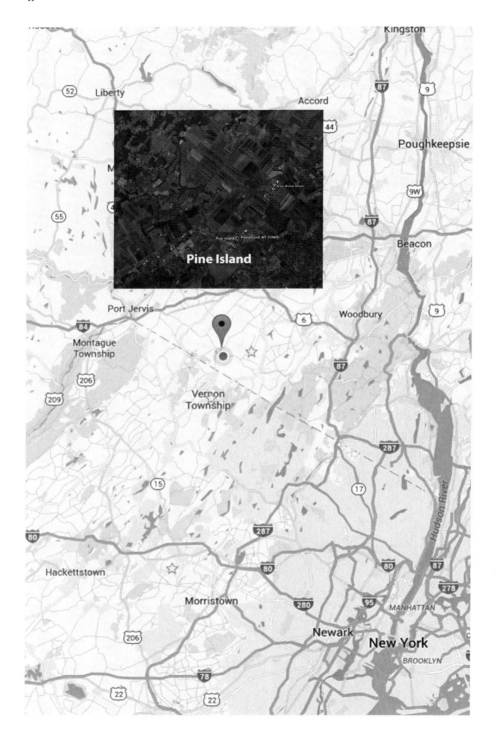

Pine Island

PREFACE

The human heart of New York State's "Black Dirt" region is Pine Island, population 2,000, a hamlet in the town of Warwick in the South-Central section of Orange County, just 60 miles from New York City.

Here, citizens live on outcrops of limestone that rise out of the fertile soil, like islands in a lake – islands in what was indeed once a massive swamp left by melting glaciers 12,000 years ago. Most Pine Islanders are farmers or connected to farming, people enticing out of the crumbly muck lands the onions, lettuce, radishes, cabbages, carrots, corn, pumpkins, squash, and new exotic "specialty" crops that help feed the ethnically diverse and increasingly fresh-food conscious population in the nearby New Jersey-New York-Connecticut tristate region.

Part of the riches of the valley is the history of the Polish and German settler communities and their very American stories – people who came to the region poor, worked hard, raised their standard of living and became contributors to both the giant metropolitan food table and the collective immigrant story.

Those who drained these Drowned Lands of Orange County and their descendants who still live and farm in the Black Dirt valley are remarkable people. But there is a disconnect between the lives of those farming this fertile region and the growing chorus from the vast urban demographic about the importance of fresh, local food.

This is the region producing much of that same fresh, local food yet few of those who are part of the locavore clamor know about the Black Dirt farmlands; few know about the extraordinarily rich dark soil, or the lives, histories and the hardships of the people growing the nutritious vegetables that help feed the biggest mouth in America. Few are aware that the Black Dirt farmers provide more than 7,000 tons of produce annually to the East Coast swath between Boston and Washington DC – one quarter of the U.S. population. Certainly, very few know how vulnerable this region is to dire threats to its survival as an agricultural wonderland.

Neither the growing community of people who want to eat fresh, locally grown food, and support local farmers, nor their elected officials, can be expected to help this agricultural region survive – let alone thrive – if they don't even know it exists, much less its character, context or the conflicts it faces.

This book informs those people about the glorious black soil, reveals the people of the valley who farm it, explains their circumstances, corrects some of the negative assumptions about farmers and farm workers, and looks at what could be the future of the region – one that surely would be appreciated and supported by those who benefit from its bounty, if only they had more information.

ABOUT THE AUTHOR

Cheetah Haysom

Cheetah has been writing all her working life. Born in South Africa, she graduated from the University of Natal, Durban, (BA Law) and started working as a reporter for a newspaper in Cape Town. She was posted to the U.S. in 1975 as a New York-based foreign correspondent for a large group of English-language South African newspapers that opposed the apartheid regime. She covered topics from films to finance, and subsequently wrote for magazines and newspapers around the world. She has lived in Pine Island, in the heart of the Black Dirt farming region of New York State, for 20 years, and written extensively on the region.

Cheetah was recently presented with the following awards:
• 2019 National Newspaper Association
Better Newspaper Editorial Contest

• 2018 New York News Publishers Association,
Distinguished Business Reporting Award of Excellence

Dedication

Cheetah dedicates this book to her husband, Don da Parma, who provided constant encouragement and support during the three years she worked on this book.

ACKNOWLEDGMENTS

Profound gratitude goes to those people in the Black Dirt Community and beyond who encouraged me to take on this project, and to keep going, though I have never been a farmer, an historian, an environmentalist, a geologist, an agronomist, an economist, an ag-activist or even a foodie.

The encouragement to get going on this book and answers to endless questions came from Chris Pawelski, Black Dirt onion farmer, communications expert, politico and friend, who is writing his own memoir on being a lobbyist for specialty crop growers while farming in the Black Dirt region.

It was John Ruszkiewicz, Pine Island Historian, and President of the Drowned Lands Historical Society, who continued over three years to patiently provide a solid background as well as a contemporary context for the predicament of the Black Dirt farmers.

The agricultural expertise of Maire Ullrich, Vegetable Agent for the Cornell Co-operative Extension, is a foundation of this book. She contributed endless time, tutorials on farming issues, and new ideas – always with passion and humor. In many ways, she is my co-author.

The design skills, publishing expertise and boundless generosity of Peter Lyons Hall made it possible to publish this beautifully layed out book with photographs and images that do credit to the subject, the Black Dirt region.

Gratitude also goes to the many people interviewed for this book, particularly those who gave me their precious time during busy farming seasons. Readers will meet them in the chapters that follow. Below is a list of many other people who, over the past three years, have played a valuable role in giving me information, suggestions, edits, support or help getting this book published. I apologize to anyone I have inadvertently left out.

Kathy Brieger	Shayne Haysom	Marsha Talbot
Chessie da Parma	Louise Haysom	Robin Wells
Sue Gardner	Carol Howard	Caroline Whiting
Gretchen Gibbs	Prof. Richard Hull	Vaughan Wiles
Jane Hamburger	Prof. Fred Isseks	Susan Wilk
Brenna Haysom	Meghann O'Donnell	
Elizabeth Haysom	Jonathan Talbot	

UPDATES NOTICE

Since Pride and Produce was first published in 2016 it has sold out twice. This third edition comes as some significant changes have come to the Black Dirt region. The biggest change is the arrival of CBD hemp as a crop, now grown on almost 20 farms and 700 acres – and the hemp craze grows. So significant could hemp farming become in the Black Dirt region that I have described that development in a new chapter towards the end of the book (Page 154). Other changes that have taken place across the Black Dirt region are covered in the final chapter, Updates (Page 157).

PART ONE:
THE CONTEXT

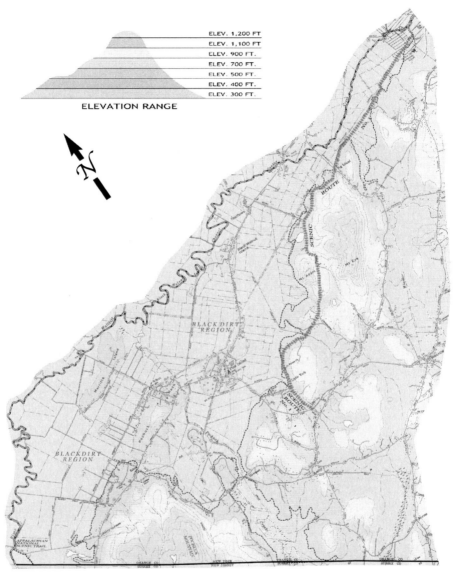

ELEV. 1,200 FT
ELEV. 1,100 FT
ELEV. 900 FT.
ELEV. 700 FT.
ELEV. 500 FT.
ELEV. 400 FT.
ELEV. 300 FT.

ELEVATION RANGE

N

BLACK DIRT REGION

BLACK DIRT REGION

LEGEND

BLACK DIRT REGION

LAKES AND PONDS

STREAMS, CREEKS AND RIVERS

CONTOUR ELEVATION

MAP NOTES:
1. MAPPING PREPARED FROM ORANGE COUNTY WATER AUTHORITY DATA.
2. NEW YORK STATE DEPARTMENT OF TRANSPORTATION PLANIMETRIC MAPS.
3. DATUM ELEVATION IS N.G.V.D. 1929.
4. MAP COMPILED AND DRAWN BY KEN R. PINKHAM / ERS CONSULTANTS, INC.
   11 FORESTER AVENUE, WARWICK, NEW YORK 10990 - (845) 987-1775.

PINE ISLAND AREA
SCALE: 1"=1000'

CHAPTER ONE: BLACK GOLD

"After the Everglades in Florida, it's the largest accumulation
of the richest soil type in the United States."

About sixty miles from New York City stretches a tract of deep, black earth, about 26,000 acres of the most fertile soil in the United States. This rich earth is an agricultural bounty, putting flavorful, nutritious and safe food on millions of tables in the most densely populated region of the United States. Yet just a handful of those who benefit from it's productivity have ever heard of this extraordinary Black Dirt valley, or know just how vulnerable is this precious asset.

Some of those who farm this dark soil refer to it as the "black gold" of the agricultural world. Indeed, it is so valued by the agricultural cognoscenti that it was long ago made illegal under New York State law to remove it from the region. But where the soil spills into neighboring New Jersey, no protective state law applies. There, deep canyons, now often filled with murky water, show where the rich black soil has been legally trucked away for private gardens.

Also known as *chernozem*, Russian for "black earth," it is found in various parts of the world including Poland, Ukraine, parts of Canada and in patches in several states, including Michigan, and further upstate New York. In Ukraine sale of the black soil is illegal. However, it is so highly valued that, according to the *Kyiv Post*, (Nov. 9, 2011) the main English language newspaper in that country, there's a $900 million annual black market in chernozem that is illicitly sold from trucks and shipped around Europe.

Even here in the Black Dirt valley so many visitors ask if they can buy the local version of chernozem to take home to their gardens out of the region that Chip Lain, an entrepreneurial sod and soybean farmer, has bought a franchise to legally mix a rich black soil from a recipe of many different fertile composts – but it is not the original muck soil, as he makes clear. He sells it by the cubic yard as "Big Yellow Bag" Black Garden Soil and delivers it to homes throughout the neighboring counties.

Fast backwards many thousands of years to a period when glaciers covered the region – in some areas as much as a mile deep. Around 12,000 years ago the glaciers began to subside, eventually leaving accumulations of boulders and glacial deposits –some of them forming "islands" in a vast murky swamp. Vegetation would grow, die, and then sink under the water which shut off air and prevented rapid decomposition. Breakdown came about through fungi and anaerobic bacteria which helps create humus.

Thousands of generations of water plants, weeds and sedges, shrubs and trees, all gradually decomposing, created layers of organic matter in the valley. Dry periods would encourage growth. They were followed by extensive flooding which helped accumulate further organic deposits developing at a rate of about 12 inches every 500 years.

Drained floodplains like the Black Dirt region of Orange County, New York, cover about 1.2 % percent of the earth's ice-free surface and are the fertile food basins for many parts of the world.

Thousands of years of flooding by the Wallkill River, which winds like a tangled brown ribbon through the plain, contributed to the continuous accumulation of organic matter in the marshland. It was known as "The Drowned Lands" until European settlers in the 1770s started the arduous, hundred-year process of draining the swamp and turning it into arable farmland.

"After the Everglades in Florida, which mainly remains a swamp, it's the largest accumulation of the richest soil type in the United States," says

Maire Ullrich, the Agricultural Program Director for Vegetable Crops at the Cornell Cooperative Extension (CCE), an agricultural outreach office in Orange County, NY. Compared with the typical topsoil depth of two to eight inches in most of the United States, the muck in the Black Dirt is between 10 and 30 feet deep. Most of the soil is 30% organic matter, some of it as much as 90%. Mineral soil farmers, (the other 98.8 %), hope for 10% organic matter, and usually accept 5%.

If you pluck a lump from the ground and put it to your nose you will detect nutty, musty tones, mushrooms, with a hint of dark chocolate – you are almost tempted to take a taste.

So black is the muck soil that it is clearly discernable from space, according to the National Air and Space Administration (NASA). From aircraft flying to and from New York's airports you can look down and recognize the black soil bordering the vast patchwork of greens - sapling green, sod green, lettuce green, celery green, soy green, arugula green … a green palette that changes through the seasons. Imagine it as a fabulous plaid, an impressionist tartan, to be worn joyfully at harvest festivals - or defiantly at official hearings on those issues that threaten the future of the family farms on this extraordinary stretch of earth.

Living amidst the Black Dirt has a rare downside. When dry, the muck soil is light and powdery so occasionally winds whip the soil into swirling dust funnels and then insinuate a layer of fine black dust into every part of our lives. In recent years most farmers have introduced low tillage practices and they grow cover crops in the spring and fall, with the result that the once notorious dust storms are now rare.

The fertility of the muck soil is only one aspect of its uniqueness. When it becomes dry it is highly combustible – farmers and farm workers are advised not to smoke while working in the fields. Fire or sparks on the surface can slip down into the soil and burn for long periods. At least one farmer is reported to have died in such a fire – he unknowingly drove his bulldozer over a patch of burning earth that collapsed beneath the vehicle's weight.

But, more helpful to farmers, the Black Dirt also retains moisture. As children of the region love to demonstrate, when they jump on the damp soil in the spring it shudders like a bowl of Jell-O. It holds nine times its mass in water, which is why it is wonderful farm soil in periods of drought. In fact, the reason that the bucolic landscape prevails throughout the valley, uninterrupted by peri-urban developments, is because these moist muck lands are very difficult to drain, and thus unsuitable for building.

Many years ago people did live in shacks on the black dirt and drank from shallow wells, even though the water stank of the sulfur in the soil. But now almost all farm barns, warehouses and homesteads are built on the uplands bordering the black soil, just as though it were still a lake. Even shacks and sheds are perched on the edge of the Black Dirt basin. A few buildings stand on gravel or dirt brought into the muck to stabilize the ground, a very expensive procedure. The soil is crumby, unstable, and has to constantly be drained by the ditches that traverse the entire valley.

Development

Quite apart from the physical qualities that rule out construction on the Black Dirt, it is illegal. The local town (Warwick) zoning forbids septic systems in the Black Dirt. And the New York State Department of Environmental Conservation Freshwater Wetlands Act forbids development of any kind on wetlands in New York State – and the Black Dirt region of Orange County is deemed to be wetlands.

There are cynics who scoff that there is no land that determined real estate developers will not find ways on which to build if there is money to be made. But the deep, soggy, bouncy, combustible, hard-to-drain characteristics of the muck soil should make it financially repellent to developers for years to come. As farmland in the Northeast continues to be removed from agriculture for development at alarming rates, the importance of preserving this region as agricultural land should become a public cause. In an era when it is Federal, State and County policy to promote preservation of farmland and to encourage people to take up farming, rezoning the Black Dirt for development would be a hard fight.

So, a little more than an hour from the skyscraper forests of Manhattan is an extraordinary treasure: 26,000 acres (25% larger than Manhattan itself) of permanent agricultural land, a perfect market garden for the growing tristate population.

Extinction Theory

While most people in the tristate region are unaware of the nearby fertile "Black Dirt" valley, the region is well known to paleontologists around the world. The soil is the repository of the bones of prehistoric animals – dinosaurs, mastodons and elk moose (a creature with features of both elk and moose) – which have been preserved deep below the surface for thousands of years. These paleontological discoveries have put Orange County and the Black Dirt region on the world map, not just for their large number but also because the region has become the geographic center of the "extinction theory."

It has long been accepted that changing temperatures – a global warming at the end of the Ice Age about 11,000 years ago, the same warming that caused glaciers to melt – led to a mass extinction of the huge Pleistocene creatures. Known as mega fauna, they included mastodons, giant sloths, lion-size beavers, native horses and camels, as well as the dire wolves and saber-toothed cats that preyed on them.

However, improvements in radiocarbon dating show that the last of the mega beasts in North America died out at the same time that a particular type of stone spear point, associated with a group known as the Clovis culture, is recorded by archeologists. Clovis artifacts dating back about 11,000 years have been found across the United States, suggesting Clovis hunters made their way across the continent.

The new, and still controversial extinction theory holds that North America's giant mammals died as a result of these human predators. It was Stone-Age hunters, not climate catastrophes that wiped them out. The chief exponent of this extinction theory is Guy Robinson, a Paleo-ecologist at Fordham University, New York, whose studies of mega fauna and plant fossils at several sites in the Black Dirt support his theory that the extinctions took place as humans arrived.

Parts of a large Pleistocene elk moose were discovered in a Black Dirt field by onion farmer Chris Pawelski and his father Rich in 2002. Five years later farm worker Rich van Sickle dug up a stag-moose as he was leveling a Black Dirt field at M & M Produce on Pulaski Highway. A collector of prehistoric relics, particularly arrow and spear heads, he recalls that he saw what looked like a piece of wood sticking out of a ditch. A few days later he returned with his brother-in-law, Luke Presley, and shovels. What they unearthed was an almost complete 11,000 year-old skeleton – only the pelvic bones and a femur are missing. The creature had an elk's body, a deer's head and the antlers of a moose. On the bones were two cut marks, raising the possibility they were wounds inflicted by Paleo-Indian spear points.

More mastodon remains have been recovered in this region than anywhere in the Northeast United States, and many more are believed still buried in the peat below the black soil. Close to the Black Dirt are the Dutchess Quarry Caves, the site where archeologists have found some of the oldest remains of Native Americans east of the Mississippi, dating back 12,000 years.

Throughout the region, but mainly on the uplands, there are relics and artifacts of the first residents of the region. They were called the "Minsi" or Minisink – which means wolf, by some accounts, and "islands" by others. The Black Dirt creeps up to the borders of the town called Minisink. These Minsi were part of the Lenape tribe who were connected to the Algonquin nation whose base was near the town of Newburgh near the Hudson River in Orange County.

For almost all the years that Native Americans inhabited the region it was a great watery swamp and the islands were reached by boat. Professor Richard Hull, Warwick Historian and author of *People of the Valleys, 1700-2005*, writes that they lived by fishing and hunting the profusion of bird and wildlife, and cultivated small gardens with a wide range of vegetables. "In The Drowned Lands," he writes, "they found huge eels, beaver and an abundance of muskrat that were valued for the fabrication of clothing."

Prof. Hull describes the Minsi as a democratic, egalitarian tribe. They were also spiritual people who revered a supreme deity along with lower spirits. The gradual arrival of Europeans in the 1600s didn't seem to affect them much but by the 1700s when the settlers started to arrive in bigger numbers the Native American population began to diminish. By the time of the Revolutionary War they had died, been assimilated or moved west, leaving no record, or scars on the landscape, only relics and artifacts under the soil.

Indeed, hunting for relics is a popular hobby; when the farmers have tilled the soil it's not unusual to see collectors bent over in the fields, scouring the upturned earth for what seem like utterly unremarkable flat grey stones – thrilling gems only to those who can recognize the subtle points and angles of an ancient arrowhead.

Drying Out the Drowned Lands

The first European settlers in the region in the early 18th century – predominantly British and Dutch – only occupied the uplands, where they raised cattle and grew fruit. They avoided farming the smelly, mosquito-infested "Drowned Lands" although, when dry enough, the swamp bed was sometimes used for cattle pasture. Sudden storms leading to rapid, unanticipated flooding could drown the grazing herds.

Although the earliest settlers in the 1770s had made efforts to drain the land it was in 1804 that serious talks began on how to drain the swamp. New York State Assembly appointed a commission to do what it could. The result was the long narrow "commissioners' ditches" which are so iconic of the Black Dirt region. These muddy furrows had limited success, so eventually in 1835 landowner General George D. Wickham constructed a drainage canal through his property to the west of the Black Dirt region.

European settlement in the region picked up when the Great Potato Famine in Ireland in 1845–49 brought large numbers of Irish to work on the railroad – initially the Goshen-Deckertown Railroad. It was first built from Goshen to a terminus in Pine Island, and then leased to the Erie Railroad, extended to Sussex, NJ, and renamed the Lehigh and New England Railroad. The combination of the railroad, completed in 1869, and the growing appetite for fresh produce in the fast expanding city of New York, gave farming a boost.

As the need for agricultural workers grew, around 1880, farmers in Orange County began to recruit the Polish immigrants and Volga Germans (who had lived beside the Volga River in Russia) who were streaming into the United States through New York to avoid religious persecution, political upheaval and grim poverty in Eastern Europe at the time. Most were country people, farm dwellers, and quite poor. Many signed on to work the farms as sharecroppers, living off a percentage of a good harvest.

These immigrants recognized the swamp bed as *chernozem* – the dark, humus-rich soil of their own home country. These were people who knew that, once drained, the oozy lake could become extremely rich farmland. Even so, it took fifty years, the construction of a canal and many ditches dug by hand to drain the valley and turn it into the most fertile farmland in the United States.

As they accumulated capital, the immigrant Polish and German farmers were able to buy parcels of land from the Irish. The Polish immigrants were almost all Roman Catholic. By 1895 there were enough of them to create a parish in the town of Florida, five miles away from Pine Island on the northwestern edge of the Black Dirt territory. The priest serving at this parish of St Joseph's negotiated for Polish farm workers to buy small parcels of a tract of 650 acres of Black Dirt land in the Pine Island region.

This tract was acreage that had come into the possession of a mission with the cumbersome name "Mission of the Immaculate Virgin for the Protection of the Homeless and Destitute Children" in the New York borough of Staten Island. It thus became known simply as The Mission Land, now one of the most intensely farmed and productive tracts in the Black Dirt region.

Initially the Mission Land tract was divided into 50-acre lots. But farming was so labor intensive that the size was far too large to farm. Many lots were divided in half, and half again. In the valley there were farms of a little more than an acre, while farms of about five acres were most common. Later, mechanization made it possible to farm larger plots, and farmers began to buy out neighbors. The farm sizes grew and grew...and still grow today. Most are farmed by the descendants of original settlers, their fields neatly delineated by the drainage ditches dug by the hands - with help of horse power - of their ancestors almost 150 years ago, and without which the region would revert to a swamp.

Due to the process of oxidation, which degrades the organic matter in the soil by an estimated 1/3 inch a year, the ground level is well below the height of the banks which border the muck lands, and lower than the roadways which traverse it, resembling causeways in a lake. Unless farmers take measures to restore the soil (which most farmers do) eventually this oxidation process will so diminish the Black Dirt it will no longer be arable.

Even though the drowned lands have been drained it's easy to half close your eyes and see the landscape as a vast green lagoon in summer, and a black lake when the dirt is freshly turned for planting in spring. Even the cottages built by the original farmers and farm workers overlooking the Black Dirt plains are reminiscent of small lakeside resort homes, many with their porches and rocking chairs facing out over the fields.

The Settler Farmers

Although many of the Polish immigrants changed their names when they passed through Ellis Island, the entry point for immigrants to the United States, names ending in "ski" (pronounced skee) dominate the tombstones in the cemetery in the heart of the hamlet. The cemetery is attached to St. Stanilaus Roman Catholic Church, where hymns and readings are sometimes still in Polish. The Polonaise Society is very active, and the

Polish Legion of American Veterans runs a social venue in the heart of the hamlet. One of the most famous sons of the region is Jimmy Sturr, who, though Irish by birth, is proudly considered the Polka King of America. Since he became a national Polka star in the early 1960s, he has won 18 Grammy Awards for his polka albums – more than anyone in a single category of music. A trumpeter, clarinetist and saxophonist, and leader of Jimmy Sturr & His Orchestra, Sturr lives in the house where he grew up in Florida, five miles down Pulaski Highway on the borders of the Black Dirt region.

Pulaski Highway is one of several roads in the region which are named for the Polish nobleman Count Casimir Pulaski, who ventured to America as a mercenary, saved the life of George Washington during the Revolutionary War and became a General in the Continental Army.

Almost every festival in the community is enlivened by the Polish dance company Pokolenie, run by fourth generation Polish farmer Joe Morgiewicz. Dancers in vivid traditional costume perform the complicated and precise steps of original Polish folk dancing – not to be mistaken for polka, which Morgiewicz says is a popular but purely American invention, never danced in Poland.

For decades the biggest Polish celebration was the famed Onion Harvest Festival held in the Black Dirt region every five years or so since 1939 until the last one, held in 1999. The festival drew Poles as well as the farming community for many miles around. Known as *Dozynki*, the Polish celebration of the harvest, the two-day cultural fair included Polish dance, music and traditional cuisine. It was at the Onion Harvest Festival in 1983 that Joe Morgiewicz – then a teenager – became determined to lead a traditional Polish dance company.

A member of a family that has been part of the foundation of the Black Dirt community, with at least 30 Morgiewicz adults still living in the region, he is a rare being – he's going back to his roots and learning to speak Polish, just as the older generation are losing their accents and forgetting the language. He says that the iconic Onion Harvest Festival has not been held for more than 15 years in part because of the enormous expense, organization of hundreds of vendors and thousands of visitors, and extensive regulation involved in such an event in modern times. And there's another factor: the gradual but ongoing dilution of the Polish community in the region.

But Poles were not the only ethnic settler group. Across a stretch of Black Dirt on the eastern side of Pine Island is Little York, an upland region where a cemetery attached to the local Evangelical Lutheran Church shows the names of Volga Germans who had lived on the banks of the Volga River in Russia and came to the United States fleeing persecution. Services there are still occasionally held in German. The settlement was called Little York because many of its early inhabitants had first settled in New York before moving here. The picturesque community is still the address of German settler families, Paffenroth, Scheuermann, Eurich, Yungman and Rudy, some of whom are still thriving Black Dirt farmers.

In the first part of the 20th Century the farms were united by one crop – the bold, pungent onion that grew very successfully in the humus-rich soil. Entire families worked the onion farms that covered almost 100% of the muck lands and became synonymous with the region. Since then many factors have forced Black Dirt farmers to abandon the region's trademark onion for different onion breeds and to grow a broad range of produce sold wholesale and retail to chain stores, grocery stores, farmers' markets, restaurants, institutions and direct to consumers throughout the New York City - New Jersey - Connecticut tristate area.

With its population of 20 million people, this locale presents one of the world's largest and wealthiest markets – figuratively, the largest collective mouth in the whole United States. Eight percent of the U.S. population lives within the region. Seven counties in this region are ranked in the top 15 jurisdictions for per capita income in the United States: New York County (Manhattan) (1), Fairfield, Connecticut (6), Somerset, New Jersey (7), Westchester, New York (10), Morris, New Jersey (11), Hunterdon, New Jersey (13), and Bergen County, New Jersey (15).

Maire Ullrich, Agricultural Program Director at the CCE, says that the Black Dirt region, with about 14,000 acres in production at present, is a part of the 88,000 farmed acres – including dairy and fruit – in all of Orange County. But its extreme fertility and its predetermined dedication to agriculture makes it an extraordinary and precious area, especially when appreciation of the nutritional and environmental value of local and fresh produce has never been greater.

Ullrich, a no-nonsense woman with a warm smile and a passion for the work she does assisting produce farmers in the region – she calls herself "the plant vet" – estimates that about 70% of the fresh produce at farmers markets in the tristate area is now grown in the Black Dirt.

This valley of rich, dark soil should be an intensively farmed and highly productive, prosperous area. After all, a local, safe supply of fresh produce is in the interest of everyone in the region. But surprisingly, there are hundreds of acres of fallow fields, much of it kept that way because of Government payments. Federal immigration (work visa) policies exacerbate a crippling farm labor shortage. The continuous flooding of the Wallkill River has destroyed entire harvests and created a sense of insecurity. Crop insurance policies, though improving, are considered inadequate for the risky climate. Regulations governing farming are strict and burdensome.

It does not help that vegetable farms are increasingly expensive to run, while American consumers, used to a bountiful supply of inexpensive food, are not keen to pay more. As a percentage of disposable income, Americans pay the least for their food of all countries in the developed world. That is not likely to change as long as the food supply and prices in the United States are controlled by a handful of megastores and chain suppliers.

The truth is that the Black Dirt is an agricultural region where many small farms are struggling after many bad years. And while some farms are worth at least a million dollars in land, warehouses, farm machinery and homes, there are few prosperous farm families. Due in part to the effects of the weather catastrophes of the past five years, some Black Dirt growers hold debts in the hundreds of thousands of dollars. The obstacles some of them face seem enough to confound their will to continue making a living from the land.

If the people who consume the produce grown in the fertile Black Dirt region are oblivious to the difficulties Black Dirt farmers face it is partly because it is in the nature of farmers to accept adversity as a factor of their livelihood and to struggle on without complaint. But it is also true that farmers throughout the region have become the objects of negative assumptions based on highly publicized mistreatment of farm workers in specific locations, mostly in Southern states. In the past, publicity – even positive reports – often led to official raids and sometimes to conduct that seemed to farm-owners as harassment. As a result farmers have avoided publicity.

But alarms might now be appropriate for the public that consumes the produce: the number of farmers in the Black Dirt dropped from about 600 in 1955 to about 60 in 1996. That number has continued to go down as children leave the farms to go into other occupations. Though farms are larger now, they number a little more 55.

Demand for the produce grown on the fertile Black Dirt fields must surely grow but if the hardships now facing farmers in the region are not resolved it is possible that, once the economy improves, more of those who are making a living from agriculture in the Black Dirt region will leave for the world of more predictable, stable, secure and profitable employment. To understand the predicament of the people who farm the region its helps to know a little about their history. ■

CHAPTER TWO: CHILDREN OF THE CHERNOZEM

"Children from Pine Island attending the Warwick Valley High School were described as hicks from the boondocks."

In the very early days farmers' children did the work in the fields. There were sometimes as many as 12 children in a family, often living in small two-bedroom houses. "Discipline was strict. It had to be," says John Ruszkiewicz, 79, a Black Dirt farmer and President of the Drowned Lands Historical Society. "I knew of a family that had a cat-o-nine tails for disciplining the kids."

Ruszkiewicz lived in the village of Florida on the edge of the muck lands until 1944 when his father moved the family to farm on the Mission Land tract in Pine Island. John, who had two brothers and a sister, was eight. "We would weed and weed and weed. Weed control was a function of how many kids you had," he recalls. "And at harvest time we would still be on our hands and knees pulling onions and clipping the tops."

A scholar-farmer, Ruszkiewicz, who is writing a history of the Mission

Lands, has degrees from Cornell and Harvard Universities and served 20 years in the Armed Forces before returning to the family farm with the rank of Lt. Colonel. He grows onions, pumpkins, soybeans and corn with his son Paul, who is an Orange County legislator.

Musing on the success of the farmers in the region in the first three decades of the 20th Century, Ruszkiewicz senior ponders how efficient and cost conscious the farmers really had to be in those days. There were no pesticides, no labor costs and no machinery to maintain – and therefore no expenses. Not just weed control, but overall success was often a function of the number of children around to work the farms.

"On the other hand, we children of those early farmers – that's my contemporaries, farmers now in their 60s to 80s - had a range of new expenses. After the late 40s technical and scientific innovations brought dramatic changes in farming. I won't use the word 'advances,'" he adds, "because it's a description that would be disputed by many. Suddenly pesticides were being used. We now had equipment to buy and maintain. And children were no longer needed. We did not use child labor like our parents did."

Ruszkiewicz remembers how the arrival of various agricultural machines changed farming, revolutionizing work that had largely been done by hand with help from horses that plodded the soggy black soil in specially made sink-resistant clogs. "There was the advent of the International Cub tractor, which was quickly adapted for a whole variety of uses in the muck lands. Then came the orange Allis-Chalmers tractor, which similarly revolutionized seeding, close cultivation and weed control. A two-row onion harvester was twinned to take on four rows. Suddenly 25 acres didn't seem like enough land."

For a while in the early 1950s celery was, alongside onions, a lucrative muck land crop and growers of both were making a very good living. "There was a saying that if you dropped a quarter in the Black Dirt in those days, by the time you picked it up it would be a dollar," Ruszkiewicz recalls.

One consequence of this success was that farm children were expected to go into farming themselves. Ruszkiewicz remembers that the neighboring Gurdas had four sons, and neighboring Bierstines had five sons, and all of the boys went on to work on their family farms. "By contrast, my father struggled as a farmer. So he sent his sons to college. Back then, farmers doing well didn't send their kids to college."

Those traditions have changed and many sons and daughters of the

Black Dirt now have graduated from college – some with post-graduate degrees. Indeed, Ruszkiewicz's son Paul, 40, is among them. "Paul was always interested in farming," recalls Ruszkiewicz senior. "I said 'first, you have to get some qualifications'." Paul did a degree in Plant Sciences followed by a Masters Degree in Farm Management and Production Economics at Cornell University, one of the top agricultural colleges in the United States. In addition to his Cornell degrees he has an Associate Degree in Agricultural Engineering from SUNY Cobleskill. Only after leaving college did he become a full time farmer, working alongside his father on their 200-acre Black Dirt fields.

As well as his college degrees, Paul Ruszkiewicz has a characteristic more typical of modern growers in the valley than the somewhat independent farmers of the old days: he is actively involved in agricultural leadership and the political community. Apart from serving as a County Legislator, Ruszkiewicz – a rather quiet, unassuming man – is President of the Orange County Vegetable Growers Association, Chairman of the Wallkill Valley Drainage District Association, a Member of the Board of the New York State Vegetable Growers Association, an active member of the Pine Island Chamber of Commerce, and serves on other boards and committees.

The farmer scholars, farmer historians, farmer social leaders, farmer politicians, and farmer entrepreneurs in the Black Dirt valley are playing an important part in their community of redefining the role of the farmer. They could also soon change the conventional view of what a farmer looks like to the broader tristate region.

Back in 1950, when there were about 600 farmers, most grew onions on about five to seven acres. Then, in 1955, there was a catastrophic flood that wiped out entire farms and demolished the spirit of those who survived. Other changes were taking place: The Ford Motor Company had built an assembly plant in Mahwah, New Jersey, just 20 miles away, where men were paid $2.80 an hour compared with the $1 they earned on the farms. The Firth Carpet Company opened in Cornwall, Orange County. And President Dwight Eisenhower fell in love with the German autobahn and began to build highways. There were jobs out there, beyond the farms. By 1956 those 600-odd farms had dropped to 300.

The history of farming in the Black Dirt is full of stories of families whose farm operations grew and grew and then collapsed. Typical was a family by the name of Gurda, original Polish settlers. "They bought everything they could," recalls John Ruszkiewicz, who is creating an oral record of the region and houses the Drowned Lands Historical Society archives in file cabinets in his farm office. Eventually, explains Ruszkiewicz, the Gurdas couldn't expand their business any further, in part because of competition from a wily, innovative farmer and entrepreneur named Vince Kosuga. One day in 1965 Kosuga, who had successfully branched into other non-farming businesses, suggested to the Gurdas that they buy him out.

He set a price and a consortium of the various Gurda family farmers jointly took on Kosuga's vast farm operations. Stanley Gurda, now 85 and the last survivor of 12 Gurda siblings, recalls that at their peak the family farmed 2,500 acres across the Black Dirt. When a series of weather calamities followed, including the dire flooding that came after Hurricane Agnes in 1972, the Gurda empire began to fail. Farm Credit initiated foreclosure in 1975 and in 1977 the Gurdas went into bankruptcy.

"There's no doubt we took on too much," said Stanley Gurda. "But it was the weather that finally did it. The quality of our crops was affected, and the prices we could get for them." From his living room in a house overlooking the 300 acres he farmed until the bankruptcy, Gurda adds that the Government was partly to blame for the harsh loan regulations enforced at the time, making it difficult for farmers to get out of debt. A few people committed suicide during those years and many left farming for the factory.

Their land was broken up and bought by many people mentioned in this book, including historian/farmer John Ruszkiewicz, whose office was once the Gurda farm office. He looks out towards the picturesque French's Island, the heart of DeBuck's Sod Farm, once Gurda property. A large portion of Gurda farmland was acquired by Ted Sobiech, a competing onion grower who himself later went into bankruptcy. However, several Gurda grand nephews, Andrew, David and Jerry, bought small plots of muck land which have now become successful agricultural operations. And two young enterprising Gurdas in their 20s are featured in the chapter on the farmers of the future.

The fall of the Gurda empire was the biggest failure, but it was not unique. There were other large crashes. They failed for a number of reasons but in most cases weather and flooding were factors. In those days, says Ruszkiewicz, farmers who had dropped out of grade school to work on the family farm had to deal with the complexities of managing a multi-million dollar operation. "Some of these operations simply became too big." Many of the large-scale growers had never had the training nor experienced the rigors that qualify Chief Executive Officers or senior management in other large businesses, he said.

Disharmony

Through the latter part of the 20th Century, many of the children of the Polish and German settler farmers, who grew up working on their family farms, stayed on to perpetuate the family business. Perhaps it was the particular work ethic that farmers passed on to their children. Maybe there's something in the magical soil that seeps into the blood through the fingers. Or, perhaps it's loyalty to the years of back-breaking work their ancestors invested in draining the Black Dirt. For whatever reason, many of the Polish and German settler families had offspring who ignored the growing call to other professions and stayed loyal to the family farm, or to the region, working in ag-related businesses.

Sons and daughters married into the community so that newspaper obituaries list surviving relatives – aunts and uncles, cousins, nieces and nephews, children and grandchildren – with the names of many of the original settler farm families. By some estimates 70% of all those Pine Islanders who have lived in the region for more than 20 years are related by blood or marriage, and often by both.

However, instead of becoming one happy, cohesive hamlet, Pine Island – and the whole Black Dirt farming region – became a community ruefully discordant. There were hostilities between neighbors, and feuds within families. "The worst thing that could happen to a Pole," explained a Pine Islander, "was for someone they knew to do better than they had done. We felt even worse," he admitted, "if it was a relative who has achieved success." This Black Dirt inversion of German *schadenfreude* (joy at another's misfortune) is explained by retired Black Dirt farmer Charlie Lain, now 85. "It was envy," he chuckles. "And it made collaboration very difficult. It almost ruined the valley."

Some of the disharmony might have resulted from that independent streak common to farmers. Maire Ullrich at the Cornell Co-operative Extension points out that for years competition between muck land farmers was particularly ferocious because they all raised the same crop, the pungent yellow onion, on a small holding, in close proximity. And since it was on flat land they could all see what their neighbors were doing.

An older farmer confided some suggestions that were currency in the valley in those days on what farmers could do "to stick it to your farm neighbor:"

1. Sell him bad seed;
2. Block the farm road;
3. Tell him you produce more per acre than he does;
4. Tell him you are getting more money for your produce than he is;
5. Give him misinformation on your weed control methods; and
6. Put out empty boxes/crates or barrels in your fields since everyone counted neighbors' containers to gauge the size of their harvest

Cheryl Rogowski, a third generation farmer of Polish heritage, recalls her father Walter, who was an onion farmer, telling her that at one point there were gentlemen's agreements between onion farmers to keep prices stable. But someone would break the accord, and trust would be destroyed. Distrust then permeated the community.

There's some animosity that remains between the Polish and German settler descendants. Stanley Gurda recalls being told that at the start of World War II when Germany invaded Poland, the sons of Polish settlers were expected to go out in to fields and fight with a German lad. But sometimes there was no hostility between the youngsters, so they would fake it, and instead of a fight they would go and share an ice cream sundae.

If there is any enmity, it might still linger in the Pine Island Fire District which is a recent union of two separate groups of firefighters, one of German descendants and one of Polish stock. They still cling to some separate cultural traditions though they serve together under the same roof and respond bravely to the same sirens.

Gurda recalls that there were some occasions of collaboration. "When the first tractors came out we didn't know how to drive them and many times people went into the ditches. Then people would come out and help each other." But the kind of communal effort, the collaboration that might have helped the region's feisty, hardworking farmers in the past troubled times, was scarce. Two attempts to get co-operation among the onion farmers failed, one in the 1930s and another in the 1990s.

There was a project in the early 1990s to brand the pungent yellow onions grown in the Black Dirt as the "Orange County Onion". With a small U.S. Department of Agriculture (USDA) grant, a logo was developed, T-

Shirts sold and someone even dressed as an onion to promote the brand. But the branding campaign didn't take off and eventually fizzled out.

Times have changed: Onion farmers now contribute to a common fund set up to promote their remarkable crop. The funds are all directed to research on growing more resistant breeds, and issues such as disease and weed control.

With the diversification of crops in the past 35 years, and new methods of reaching markets – including 54 farmers' markets scattered throughout New York City – competition between farmers has greatly diminished and a new network of growers who depend on one another and collaborate has developed. People in the Black Dirt region roll their eyes or chuckle about the feuds in their community, but they also note that in the last few years the weather catastrophes and flooding have served to unite people in organizations and committees working on ways to help the whole community survive – even prosper. And as labor shortages and new technologies have made new expensive farm machinery a solution to many problems, a growing number of farmers are getting together to share their equipment, resources, know-how and even their land.

The Wrong Side of the Tracks

This Black Dirt region stretches beyond Pine Island, which is just the hamlet at its center. The lake of black soil flows into Goshen, Florida and Chester, all far larger towns in Orange County. Pine Island itself nestles in the western edge of the town of Warwick, under whose municipal authority the hamlet falls. Warwick provides police, sanitation, roads, parks and recreation from a government building 15 minutes from the Pine Island crossroads. The current Warwick Town Supervisor, Michael Sweeton, has been attentive to the needs of the Pine Island community – he is even a regular contestant in the annual Pine Island Chamber of Commerce raw onion-eating contest. After all, beside education and healthcare, agriculture – including apples and dairy farmed on regular brown soil – is the only "industry" in the Warwick Valley.

But in spite of the bucolic landscapes and rich immigrant history, the people of Warwick, and particularly the picturesque, somewhat gentrified village of Warwick at the heart of the Town, long regarded Pine Island as "the wrong sides of the tracks." Going back about 40 years, farmer Cheryl

Rogowski recalls, children from Pine Island attending the Warwick Valley High School were described as "hicks from the boondocks." Several Pine Islanders said that as children they would often pretend they lived in Warwick Village, rather than admit to being a Pine Islander. The disregard for Pine Island kids was reversed, however when it came to picking lads for the Warwick High School football team. The Pine Island boys, who helped on the farms from the time they were little kids, were strong and hardy and considered very desirable as school team athletes.

Back in the 1960s when Pine Island farmers were prosperous, the Lincoln Continental was their automobile of choice. Over at the Warwick Country Club one night a Warwick local was heard to announce at the bar that he'd decided to sell his Lincoln Continental. The reason, he said, was "people think I come from Pine Island."

Pine Island Elementary School was outstanding, with the highest grades in the Warwick school system, and high rankings in the Ulster-Dutchess-Orange County region. Yet, when the Warwick Valley Central School District had a critical budget shortfall in 2011, the Pine Island Elementary School was closed, a shocking blow to the community. There was little objection to the closing of the school from the Warwick community.

Pine Island was originally part of Goshen, the County seat. It became part of Warwick Town in 1779. Today, the town of Warwick, (pop 30,000) includes the Villages of Greenwood Lake and Florida, the Village of Warwick, and the hamlets of Amity, Bellvale, Edenville, Greenwood Forest Farms, Pine Island, Little York, New Milford, and Sterling Forest. In the past 30 years the Warwick Valley has become an increasingly upscale, affluent area, filled with restaurants, antique and gift stores and meticulously preserved historic sites. Warwick has the charm and facilities of any town in Connecticut's millionaires' belt, without the steaming property prices.

Property inflation has been stalled in part because Warwick is not an easy commute to New York City. The only public transport for commuters to Manhattan is the New Jersey Transit bus service, and trains that run from stations at least 20 minutes away. The Warwick local authority has fought vigorously for years to control development, keep out box stores, and preserve a picturesque and commercially viable Main Street.

The village of Warwick is also host to the annual Applefest, named one of the "Top 100 Events" in the country by the American Bus Association. It was started in 1989 as a simple harvest celebration to support the Warwick

Valley Community Center. More than 30,000 visitors now attend the one-day event, enjoy the range of Warwick's apples, country town atmosphere, and musical entertainment. Warwick's standing as an "undiscovered gem" is slowly changing, helped by the March 2014 listing of Warwick as one of the ten best weekend getaways in America by StyleCaster, a popular national online network. It won the accolade "Most Beautiful Village in the World" by the Communities in Bloom International Challenge in 2010. And the local county newspaper, the *Times Herald-Record*, gave its 2015 Reader's Choice Awards to Warwick as the "Best Place to Spend the Day Shopping."

Pine Island, by comparison, has remained an unpretentious farming outpost, see-sawing between near bust and mini-boom according to the weather and the market exigencies that dominate farming life today. Prejudices against Pine Island have been exacerbated by rumors that the air is filled with chemicals used for farming, and the water is polluted by pesticide runoff.

Marsha Talbot, a realtor with Rand Realty in Warwick, who lives in a country farmhouse in Amity, next to Pine Island, points out that realtors are required by New York State and local law to inform prospective buyers of property in agricultural areas that the region has all the manifestations of farm life – slow moving vehicles at rush hour, tractors growling through the fields pre-dawn, and pesticides in the fields from time to time. An "Agricultural Districts/Farming Disclosure" must be signed by buyers and sellers.

The presence in Pine Island of migrant farm workers – mainly from Central America and Mexico – has also aroused assumptions about the region. One story was that Latino children attending the Pine Island Elementary School were diminishing the quality of education because they could not speak English. On the contrary! As pointed out earlier, the Pine Island Elementary School, a proud red brick building atop the highest hill in Pine Island, had the best grades in the Warwick school system. Under an outstanding school principal, Jane Hamburger, the migrants' children (about 5% of the population) were treated as a very special asset, a treasured testament to the hamlet's agricultural legacy. Hamburger used the farm environment as an educational tool to teach children about science, culture, history and integrity.

Hamburger recalls that when she became principal in 1989 the Pine Island school would be given the old furniture and equipment that was being replaced in other schools in the district. It was the same with text books. There was a book in the library called "Someday Man May Walk on the Moon."

"What I did, over time," says Hamburger, "was to fight for equity in programs, facilities, supplies, and equipment. Working in collaboration with a staff that I had almost entirely hired, our students began to catch up and then exceed the other district schools and those in the tri-county area." The school building, now a partly unoccupied brick structure overlooking the hamlet, still serves as a monument to the bitterness in Pine Island over the forced closing of their beloved elementary school.

Prejudices, both in Pine Island and in Warwick, also led to the Donald Trump-like assumption that the migrant farm workers would be responsible for crime in the region. Wrong again! Town Supervisor Michael Sweeton reports that the Black Dirt region around Pine Island boasts the lowest crime rate of the entire Town of Warwick.

Uncertainty about Pine Islanders might have arisen from society's often ambivalent attitude towards farmers: are they uneducated folks who abuse their farm workers? Are they the new-age earth-people, those special hard working humans whose hands in the ground magically put healthy food on our tables? Are they post-grad foodies who understand the best modern growing practices, market demands, nutrition and how to whip up a dandelion root stir-fry? The attitudes range from ignorance to mystical reverence.

Isolation

Warwick's attitudes towards Pine Island over the decades may have reinforced the independence in the community as a whole, and served to keep it somewhat isolated. A Pine Island Polish resident recalls that until fairly recently it was frowned on to marry outside the Pine Island community. In 1965 Black Dirt onion farmer Rich Pawelski, third generation Polish, married Grace Kurtz, from Warwick. She moved into his farmhouse on a pretty tree-studded island rising out of the muck land off Pulaski Highway.

"I really had a hard time being accepted," she says, "because I wasn't Polish." It didn't matter that she was at the time a devout Catholic and had become a member of St. Joseph's Catholic Church. What the Pawelskis saw as theological hypocrisy led them to leave the Catholic Church.

Today, attitudes towards Pine Island's children in the Warwick public school have changed. As the population has grown, the percentage of Pine Islanders who are farmers has dropped. But more importantly, respect for farmers has grown, not just in the Warwick Valley but in the nation as a whole. Remember the gauzy Dodge Ram advertisement during Super Bowl XLVII, a devotion to the American farmer? Warwickians are increasingly a part of that demographic that seeks out local, fresh, nutritious food and admires those who produce it. The farmers' market in Warwick on Sundays throughout the summer attracts between 900 and 1,300 people, from the town and beyond. Most of the produce vendors are from the Black Dirt region.

After the catastrophic floods that followed Hurricane Irene and laid waste to almost the entire 2011 Black Dirt harvest, the people of the Town of Warwick rallied. They quickly put together a fundraiser at the Warwick Valley High School, raising $100,000 for devastated farmers. Food donations and fundraising efforts for farm workers, left without income, continued through spring 2012, when planting brought back jobs and income.

The rich, rare soil, the extraordinary pre-history of the muck lands and the tales of the hardy European settlers who drained it, are all of growing value to the whole Warwick valley. There is a new recognition that the Black Dirt farmland is an integral and increasingly important part of the region. And the celebrated pungent onion, so closely associated with the region, is a large part of the story. ▨

CHAPTER THREE: THE ONION CAPITAL OF THE WORLD

"I can't think of anything more important in the kitchen –
except perhaps heat and water."

In the 1930s Pine Island became known for the crop that was grown across almost 100% of the muck lands for more than 50 years. Plants of the species *Allium Cepa* that originated in Central Asia, onions have spread all over the world in hundreds of varieties. The first to plant onions in the muck lands may have been a small group of Irish who settled in Durlandville, which became known as "Little Dublin." A few farm lanes in the region still bear Irish names. So successful was this crop in the humus-rich sulfurous soil that it soon became the single crop of the Polish and German settler farmers who followed the Irish.

A sign erected by the Chamber of Commerce in Pine Island in the 1960s proudly proclaimed the hamlet to be "The Onion Capital of the World." It was cute hyperbole, of course. The largest onion producer in the world is China, and the largest consumer is India, where eating an onion is almost a religious rite. Indeed, riots have followed onion shortages in India. Pine Island, in reality, was the center of the largest onion-producing region in New York State and at the peak of production the region was growing a sixth of the onions grown in the United States. In those nostalgic days the pungent onion of the Black Dirt fetched good prices and made many farmers quite well off.

What is not hyperbole – though barely known – is that the gold colored yellow globe onions grown in the Black Dirt are exceptional, with the best flavor and possibly the greatest health benefits of any onions grown in the United States. Although you don't hear them ranked among the trendy "super foods," they are nutritious, they have healing qualities and they are supremely tasty, with the ability to enhance the flavor of the dreariest dishes. The benefits of the muck land onions are a result of the soil in which they are grown, the basin of compost that contains between 30 and 50 percent humus – and in some areas as much as 90 percent.

Know Your Onions

The high sulfur content in the soil makes them among the most pungent onions on the market, and that quality also makes them among the most flavorful when cooked – not just full of the oniony flavor that enriches stews and soups, but also more sugars that make them the best for caramelizing on the stove. All these culinary assets are not just cooks' observations, they are lab-proven facts.

What is laughable is that recipes from lauded chefs and food writers often call for the sweet onions – "Granex" varieties such as Vidalia, Maui, Walla Wall, Imperial Valley – for cooking, when in fact exposure to heat renders them almost tasteless. Knowledgeable cooks recommend Granex onions for eating raw.

As food writers Matt Lee and Ted Lee wrote in *The New York Times* (Oct 24, 2007) after a visit to the Black Dirt:

> *Although Granex onions have a reputation for sweetness —*
> *You can eat them like an apple" goes the old saw —*
> *that's because they contain more water and significantly*
> *less pyruvic acid. Orange County yellow onions contain*
> *nearly as much sugar but because they have less water, they*
> *caramelize more readily in the pan. These onions also stay*
> *firm longer after an intense fry or a long, slow roast. Their*

flavor mellows nicely with cooking, the ample sugars are
revealed, and their wonderfully brassy flavor is preserved.

Darryl Mosher, Assistant Professor at the Culinary Institute of America at Hyde Park, NY, where he is an expert on produce, said of the cooking onion: "I can't think of anything more important in the kitchen – except perhaps heat and water." Mosher, who is also a produce farmer with a small holding in Dutchess County, NY, said sweet onions were appropriate for sandwiches and salads and perhaps a quick stir fry. "The two types have the same amount of sugar, but the sugar in the cooking onion is more accessible when heated. The sulfur component gives it a depth of flavor. Cooking masks the acids and enzymes and allows the characteristic onion flavors to come through."

The pungent juice of onions has been used as a moth repellent and can be rubbed on the skin to prevent insect bites. When applied to the scalp it is said to promote growth of hair and on the face to reduce freckles. It has been used to polish glass and copperware and to prevent rust on iron. If boiling water is poured onto chopped onions and left to cool, the resulting liquid can be sprayed onto plants to increase their resistance to pests, and the onion plants when growing are reputed to keep away certain rodents and bugs. Onion skins have been used to produce dyes.

But there is one unpopular sulfur component in the onion: the "lachrymator," which causes eyes to water. Harold McGee writes about it in his famous book for serious cooks *On Food and Cooking: The Science and Lore of the Kitchen*:

> *This volatile chemical escapes from the damaged onion into the*
> *air, and lands in the onion cutter's eyes and nose, where it*
> *apparently attacks nerve endings directly….Its effects can be*
> *minimized by pre-chilling the onions for 30-60 minutes in ice*
> *water. This treatment slows the ammunition-breaking enzyme*
> *down to a crawl, and gives all the volatile molecules less energy*
> *to launch themselves into the air. It also hydrates the papery onion*
> *skin, which makes it tougher and less brittle, and so easier to*
> *peel off the skin.*

Maire Ullrich of CCE, an expert on all matters onion, recommends cutting with a very sharp knife, thus minimizing the number of cells that are crushed.

Apart from their culinary superiority, the Black Dirt golden onions have no fat or cholesterol, are highly nutritious and come with proven health benefits. The sulfur in the black soil, which contributes to the high pyruvic acid content, is a blood thinner, helps to increase circulation and prevents heart disease. These onions also contain cancer-preventing anti-oxidants and are recommended by the Arthritis Foundation for anti-inflammatory benefits.

In the Arthritis Foundation journal *Arthritis Today*, writer Linda Richards repeated the onion's health benefits.

> *Onions are also one of the richest sources of flavonoids – antioxidants that mop up free radicals in your body's cells before they have a chance to cause harm. One flavonoid found in onions, called quercetin, has been shown to inhibit inflammation-causing leukotrienes, prostaglandins and histamines in osteoarthritis (OA) and rheumatoid arthritis (RA), reduce heart disease risk by lowering low-density lipoprotein (LDL) or "bad" cholesterol and help prevent the progression of cancer.*

She adds that one of its powerful compounds has been shown to inhibit the breakdown of bone, working in the same way as drugs like Fosamax, which are used to treat osteoporosis.

No scientific evidence exists to support the other health theories about the onion – that it fights chronic bronchitis, hay fever and asthma. Aphrodisiac qualities are also attributed to onions in India, where – as is the case throughout the rest of the world – the onions eaten are pungent varieties, not sweet onions.

In the view of some in the marketing and branding businesses, the Black Dirt onion, with its many culinary and health qualities, should be among the most prized of produce. But these golden gems are treated as ignominious extras. They are usually sold in two, three and five pound mesh bags in supermarkets on the east coast, where they fetch about $2.50 for six to eight baseball sized onions. Nothing in packaging or store labeling indicates they are full of benefits or that they come from the Black Dirt. The onion bag might mention Pine Island, or the other towns in the Black Dirt region, Florida, Goshen and Chester, but a speck or two of black soil might be the only evidence of their superiority.

Why no branding campaign, no clever trademark, no promotional slogan to burnish the image of the Black Dirt onions, enrich the regions farmers and enlighten the public – not to mention enhance public health?

After all, pungent onions were the most popular type throughout the U.S.. In 1950 100% of onions consumed in the U.S. were pungent varieties. But by 2000 the figure was 50%. Preferences began to shift in the 1980s when the United States discovered that seductive sweet southern belle, the Vidalia onion. About that time, everything in the United States onion market changed, and the "Onion Capital," lost its title.

Sissy versus Sassy

Vidalia onions are a selection of mild types, due to the low sulfur content in the soil where they are grown. First planted near Vidalia, Georgia, in the early 1930s, production spread to 14 counties. In 1986 Georgia's state legislature passed the "Vidalia Onion Act" which authorized a trademark for "Vidalia Onions" and limited production to Georgia. All the marketing and branding tricks for the Vidalia added up to the most successful campaign in the history of vegetable production. Even children were targeted. One season the Vidalia purloined the popular movie character Shrek with the slogan "Shrek Forever After, Vidalia's Forever Sweet." Even a song was written for the Vidalia: The 1999 album *OH! The Grandeur*, by American musician Andrew Bird includes an ode to the Southern onion.

The success of the Vidalia promotion made it so trendy that consumers believed it was *haute cuisine* and bought it for cooking. The Vidalia's popularity increased the market for all sweet onions with the result that the production and sales of a range of others soared. Texas Sweets, Walla Wallas from Washington State and the California Sweets swamped the market forcing pungent onion producers here and everywhere to tear up.

Black Dirt onion farmer John Ruszkiewicz says there are reasons for which local onion growers can thank the Vidalia campaign. For one, sweet onions did not leave "onion breath." As the popularity of sweets grew the association in the public consciousness of onions with bad breath almost completely disappeared. And people came to realize that eating onions raw was not so bad after all.

At about the same time that the sweet onion hit the market, the American public began to eat out more – mainly at fast food restaurants. The demand for larger onions for institutional use swelled. The milder red onion, great for eating raw on a burger, replaced some of the demand for yellow pungents. The market had dramatically changed.

Onions are a basic ingredient in most of the major cuisines of the world except Japanese. Processed onion, mainly as powder, is the third most common food additive after salt and sugar. The growing popularity of ethnic food has increased the consumption of onions in the United States from nine pounds a person a year in the 1950s, to about 28 pounds today. But only in the U.S. is there such a high market for sweet onions.

Understandably, dissing the sweet Vidalia is a wry pastime in the Black Dirt region. It is called "wussy" and "waterball." The battle between the two is dubbed sissy versus sassy. But there is no dissing the Vidalia marketing campaign. Perhaps Black Dirt onion farmers might have been able to influence consumers' choices by educating them about the pungent yellows.

There might have been an opportunity in 1999 when a small band of upstate onion farmers growing yellow pungents in a stretch of black soil much like the Black Dirt of Orange County but far shallower, created a brand identity. With the help of a Syracuse advertising agency these Oswego County growers named their onions "New York Bold" and adopted the slogan "Onions with Attitude," registering their own LLC under that name. Using Federal and State grants and private money, they launched a campaign to promote their own New York onions –the ones grown in Oswego County.

They controlled the trademark, and the excluded Black Dirt farmers were furious, particularly because funds for a statewide promotion had not included them. (Later, when there were bumper onion crops and the price dropped, the New York Bold, with its higher "premium brand" prices, had trouble selling.)

After the New York Bold campaign took off without them, some Black Dirt onion growers talked of a new campaign that would be truly statewide, and give brand identity to all the New York farmers producing pungent muck land onions. But there was no consensus that "banding together and branding together" could work. The idea lapsed.

Whatever the reasons for the failure to brand the Black Dirt onion, some of the Black Dirt onion packers are resented because of the wholesale price they pay growers – a price dictated by the retail outlets, mainly chain supermarkets like Shoprite and Walmart. The price paid to the growers is sometimes so low farmers make just a few cents per pound. In spite of all the wonderful qualities of the Black Dirt onions they remain 'dirt' cheap. Until 2014, which was an unusually good year for Black Dirt onion growers, the first in many, farmers were paid roughly 17cents a pound for a vegetable that costs them about 16 cents a pound to produce, and was fetching about $1.50 per pound in the produce shelves, a price that had barely increased in the past 20 years. The bonanza 2014 crop fetched farmers as much as 20c a pound at the start of the harvest, though prices dropped again by the end of the summer.

The supermarkets also set the size of the onions they will accept. Once, the minimum diameter was 1-¾ inches. The standard now is 2 to 2 1/4 inches in diameter – so big that not all the onion is likely to be used at one meal. The rest will be junked. "There's a new rumor going around that if you save a cut onion in your fridge it collects and spreads bacteria," laughs Chris Pawelski, an onion farmer. "So people feel obliged to throw the unused part away."

In fact, the opposite is true. Among its medicinal qualities, the onion kills bacteria, which is why it has been used as an antiseptic to heal open wounds on battlefields (including during the Civil War). It is so powerful a killer of bacteria that it will not ferment – to the dismay of those who have tried to capitalize on all that onion sugar to make onion wine.

The larger size standard hurts the farmers because it requires that they grow a variety that remains in the ground longer. Most farmers grow an onion that reaches maturity in 115 days. The greater the period it is in the soil, the more vulnerable it is to disease. This increases the cost of "protection" from all the enemies of the onion in the field. Further, larger onions must be planted further apart, which diminishes the size of the crop and makes the fields more vulnerable to weeds. Onions that don't meet the supermarkets' size standard are unacceptable and must be sold to second tier, lower paying outlets, or trashed.

In hard years, when the weather conditions lead to a crop of onions that is damaged, or far smaller than supermarkets' absolute standards, hundreds of thousands of onions are returned to the fields to rot. In poor years mounds of perfectly edible small onions, or those with a slight nick or imperfection, lie piled in the fields, and the aroma of rotting onions pervades the Black Dirt valley.

To help make ends meet – if not overlap a little – some creative farmers have considered processing their onions to increase their value – chopped, frozen onions, and onion chips. Russell Kowal, one of the few farmers who was dedicated exclusively to growing onions, wondered if there was a place for onion cereal. He was making a point about how far afield growers are roaming in their consideration of ways of making the onions a bit more profitable. Russ says that over the past 30 years many onion growers had to switch from the original golden globes to hybrids that have a longer shelf life, which is important to retailers, and are more pest and disease resistant, which cuts costs.

He points out that producing onions in the Black Dirt today is expensive – between $3,000 and $5,000 an acre for pesticides, labor and gas for farm equipment. Like the majority of Black Dirt farmers, Russ works at other jobs so he can continue farming and pay the bills. The vast majority of America's family farms have an outside source of income.

The tough market for onions and the disastrous weather that whacked the Black Dirt region in the past three decades induced many farmers to give up. Only five are now dedicated solely to onions. While most mixed-crop growers often include onions in their basket of produce very few grow the original Black Dirt pungent onions that made the region famous. However, the fertile soil has not only welcomed new onion varieties that are more resistant to bugs and disease and have a longer shelf life, it has nurtured a wide range of vegetables that farmers have planted since crop diversification started about 35 years ago. Farmers now grow a broad range, including cabbage, radishes, cucumbers, eggplant, pumpkins, squash, lettuce and sweet corn. They are also experimenting with exotics and produce specially grown for ethnic markets – mainly Asian and Hispanic. One Black Dirt farmer grows vegetables exclusively for the Swedish market.

Not all the surviving muck land farmers switched to produce crops. In 1966 Charlie Lain, one of the few farmers in the area who does not have Eastern European heritage, took over a small plot of land, 15 acres that had once nurtured onions, and planted turf grass. Charlie's sod farm grew to about 600 acres. It was bought by his son Chip, and is now a swathe of green sod and soybeans that flanks the Wallkill River. They provide lush turf for parks, schools, public fields and lawn projects from Southern New Jersey north to Massachusetts. Green natural turf grass is among the few Black Dirt crops today that aren't grown for consumption. But compared with visually harsh asphalt and black top, it is food for the eyes and nourishment for the soul.

Onions are New York State's third most successful vegetable crop, after cabbage and corn and the onion is in a close contest with corn to be named the official state vegetable.(Technically, corn is a grain, not a vegetable, but sweet corn is deemed a vegetable.) Half the state's onions – about $20 million worth – are grown on 5,200 acres of Black Dirt. The region is still mainly associated with onions. But farmers are growing a wide variety of vegetables and herbs and many are gaining some celebrity – even a sort of agri-stardom- in New York farmers' market and restaurant circles. Indeed, when the extraordinary fertility of the soil and the wide range of crops it nurtures becomes fully recognized, that old Chamber of Commerce sign stored away with relics and artifacts from the region's past might well be retrieved and edited to proclaim a new hyperbole: "The Produce Capital of the World." ■

CHAPTER FOUR: THE ONION KING

"…a nice guy when he wasn't ruining people on the onion market."

Those who knew Vince Kosuga (1915 –2001) recall that for all his enormous stature in the farming community, he was a small man, about five feet four inches tall, who wore red-tinted sunglasses and is reputed to have carried a .38 caliber handgun and a billy club. Though his name, more than any other, is associated with onions and the Black Dirt region, attitudes towards him range from admiration and gratitude to anger and bitterness.

The Gantz brothers Eddie (74) and Richard (72) of Gantz Farm Service in Slate Hill, who knew Kosuga well all their adult lives, recall him as a man of extraordinary generosity who would pay friends' debts or medical bills, help people get set up in business and introduced a range of technical advances that transformed farming in the region.

They describe Kosuga as a man of great accomplishment as a farmer, an entrepreneur, a businessman, a real estate investor and a philanthropist. They consider his detractors as people jealous of his accomplishments and wealth. But as finance writer Emily Lambert explains in *The Futures: The Rise of the Speculator and the Origins of the World's Biggest Markets* (2010), Vince Kosuga was also a ruthless man who changed onion trading forever.

The child of a Polish immigrant and of a Russian Jew who converted to Catholicism, he grew up in Pine Island and graduated from S.S. Seward High School in Florida, NY, with academic distinction. He did many jobs as a youngster – shining shoes among them. He was already buying and selling onions at the age of 14.

In 1937 he married Pauline "Polly" Paffenroth, daughter of German immigrants living in Little York, creating one of the many unions that joined the Poles and Germans who settled the Black Dirt islands. Polly was his partner in all his ventures and it was for her that he chose his "Polly-K" trademark.

By 1940 Kosuga had enough money to buy his first 12.5 acre plot in the muck lands and was farming a range of produce. Then he started trading wheat futures, which went badly and almost bankrupted him. He left commodity trading and returned to his Black Dirt farm. But Kosuga found the allure of trading powerful and in 1955 he returned to Chicago to trade in onion futures – onions being the most-traded product on the Mercantile Exchange at the time. Kosuga spent half his time in Pine Island, and half in Chicago, where he had great success and his largesse became legendary. One year, the story goes, he gave a new Buick to each of his brokers.

Emily Lambert reports in her book that Kosuga sometimes used deceptive practices to manipulate the futures market. She says he once bribed a weather bureau to issue a frost warning in order to inflate the price of futures contracts that he owned. The weather bureau broadcast the warning, although the temperature never dropped below 50 °F.

Lambert describes how, with Sam Seigel, a fellow onion trader and owner of a local produce company, Kosuga hatched a plot to corner the onion futures market. It was the fall of 1955, the year of the catastrophic flood in the muck lands and Kosuga may have seen it as an opportunity. The two men bought so many onions and onion futures that they controlled 98 percent of the available onions in Chicago.

"Millions of pounds of onions were shipped to Chicago to cover their purchases. By late 1955, they had stored 30,000,000 pounds (14,000,000 kg) of onions in Chicago. They soon changed course and convinced onion growers to begin purchasing their inventory by threatening to flood the market with onions if they did not. Seigel and Kosuga told the growers that they would hold the rest of their inventory in order to support the price of onions.

"As the growers began buying onions, Seigel and Kosuga purchased short positions on a large amount of onion contracts. They also arranged to have their stores of onions reconditioned because they had begun to spoil. They shipped them outside of Chicago to have them cleaned and then repackaged and re-shipped back to Chicago. The new shipments of onions caused many futures traders to think that there was an excess of onions and further drove down onion prices in Chicago.

"By the end of the onion season in March 1956, Seigel and Kosuga had flooded the markets with their onions and driven the price of 50 pounds (23 kg) of onions down to 10 cents a bag. In August 1955, the same quantity of onions had been priced at $2.75 a bag. So many onions were shipped to Chicago in order to depress prices that there were onion shortages in other parts of the United States.

"Seigel and Kosuga made millions of dollars on the transaction due to their short position on onion futures. At one point, however, 50 pounds (23 kg) of onions were selling in Chicago for less than the bags that held them. This drove many onion farmers into bankruptcy. A public outcry ensued among onion farmers who were left with large amounts of worthless inventory. Many of the farmers had to pay to dispose of the large amounts of onions that they had purchased and grown."

Vince Kosuga was condemned widely for what he'd done, but he didn't appear to care. "If it's against the law to make money...then I'm guilty," he told his critics.

The Commodity Exchange Authority launched an investigation and the U.S. Senate Committee on Agriculture and House Committee on Agriculture held hearings on the matter. Kosuga had to testify before congress, where he defended what he had done. During the hearings, the Commodity Exchange Authority said that the perishable nature of onions made them vulnerable to price swings. Then Congressman Gerald Ford of Michigan sponsored the Onion Futures Act, which banned futures trading in onions. The bill was not popular among traders but it was passed and President Dwight D. Eisenhower signed it in August 1958. Thanks to Kosuga, Onions are the only commodity for which futures trading is banned in the United States.

Kosuga returned to his farm in the Black Dirt and focused on his local business interests and philanthropy. By the mid 1960s he owned 1,500 acres, most of it in the Pine Island area, and was farming lettuce, celery and onions. He was now known as "The Onion King" – perhaps he was indeed the largest onion farmer in the country at one time.

He had a profound impact on farming in the Black Dirt region because of his endless innovation in a conservative world. Ignoring the local farming traditions he tried new techniques, fertilizers, and crop strains. Some of the legends surrounding Vince Kosuga involve the machinery he invented or introduced. He brought the first rototiller to the region in 1950 and invented a "mechanical mule" to take newly picked produce, wash it and pack it in the field. He helped design a ditch digger and built dikes to hold back the floodwaters in the valley.

Kosuga tackled the storage problem faced by all truck farmers by building a vast bulk storage facility and a five-story jet vacuum cooler on Transport Lane – the first in the region. In fact the mechanization and innovations Kosuga brought to the region are credited with advances that spread throughout the Black Dirt farming region. While his farm operations were growing, Kosuga branched out, at one time running 26 different companies, including the Victory Speedway in nearby Middletown, construction businesses and commodity trading. For fun, he drove stock cars, and as a licensed pilot he flew planes.

The Kosugas eventually sold their farm to the Gurda family, their main competitors in the Black Dirt, in 1965, but continued their other business operations. They gave land for a number of community causes, including St. Peter's Lutheran Church in Pine Island, and the American Legion in Chester. Kosuga paid for extensive improvements to St. Stanislaus Roman Catholic Church in Pine Island, and made donations to hospitals in the area.

Kosuga's contributions extended far beyond the Black Dirt. He received a citation from the U.S. Government for helping to provide fresh food to the U.S. armed forces in World War II, and received a Certificate of Appreciation from the Vietnam War Veterans Coalition for his work for the organization.

A popular young blogger named Karl Smallwood recently read about Kosuga and was so intrigued by his story he wrote *"The Most Evil Businessman in History was an Onion Farmer"* ("In Fact Fiend," August 5, 2013). About a year later he dedicated another blog to a more balanced view of the Black Dirt Icon in which he said Kosuga was: "…a nice guy when he wasn't ruining people on the onion market." (*"I Found Out,"* April 23, 2014). A nice guy or not, unflattering stories about him abound in the community.

The Kosugas were devout Roman Catholics. Polly Kosuga said in a telephone interview that the most significant events in their many years together were their three papal audiences. "Our meetings with the popes were the highlights of our lives."

By the time he died in 2001 Vince Kosuga was appreciated by many in the region. Almost 50 years had past since his notorious trading days. Polly, who had always been regarded with affection by the community, remained loyal to the Kosuga principle of philanthropy until she died in 2009.

Among the Pine Island landmarks that are prominent reminders of the Kosuga role in the community is a housing development off Kosuga Lane in the heart of the hamlet. As part of the deal with the zoning board to build the Kosuga Lane development, Kosuga ceded a patch of land he owned nearby to the town to become public space – what is now the popular Pine Island Park.

But Kosugas' best known legacy was Ye Jolly Onion Inn, the legendary restaurant at the crossroads, which the couple founded in 1961. First it was a pit stop for the many truckers moving produce out of the area. Then Polly and Vince, who loved cooking, expanded the eatery into a serious restaurant that brought distinction to the region. "The Jolly," with its cartoon sign showing a smiling onion, became famous – one of the most popular eateries in the area – drawing customers from counties around.

It was bought by German immigrants Hans Gross and Walter Greiner in 1971. They recreated it as a German-American restaurant and attracted customers with hearty country fare. The business was taken over by the Greiner's sons Walter and Jeff. They kept the traditional German-American fare and regular customers.

But new culinary sensibilities swept through the U.S. in the 2000s, including *nouvelle cuisine* portion size and an adventurousness about ingredient combinations that was not part of The Jolly's traditional style. The restaurant's decor was beginning to age. Just when it seemed Ye Jolly Onion Inn had to change or die, a local businessman bought the restaurant and building. He basically tried to keep it as it was, perhaps in response to admonitions within the community not to change anything. But customers continued to fall off and within a year the doors had closed. Ye Jolly Onion Inn belonged to a bank.

The iconic restaurant site in Pine Island has been empty since 2007, casting a pall over the heart of the hamlet. The property was bought in 2012 by a partnership: Andy Field, a successful real estate developer with existing properties in Pine Island, and Will Brown, an economist who raises grass-fed cattle, sheep, and pigs on 300 acres in the Pine Island area. In 2015 two businesses opened in the lower sections of the building, a hair salon and a popular market for antiques and upscale second hand trinkets. As for the old site of the eatery, both men are committed to finding investors with plans that will tie in with the agricultural character of the region. And on the large Jolly Onion sign at the Pine Island crossroads, the cartoon onion still shows an optimistic smiley face.

But the kind of stardom once associated with the Onion King Kosuga has long gone. Today's star farmers are a new breed, men and women who grow a range of crops, deal with very different issues and shine in totally different orbits. ■

CHAPTER FIVE: ROCK STAR FARMERS OF THE MUCK LANDS

"At the end of the day, the farmer is such an intrinsic part of the American psyche it is natural for them to be rock stars next." - M. Batali

The modern urban foodie movement in America has declared that farmers are the new rock stars. If that means they are wildly popular, hugely successful, and widely recognized for their contribution to our lives – well, not yet. But many of the farmers of the Black Dirt are indeed stars. And though they seldom play the same tune, they have tremendous individual style. Here are just a few.

Cheryl Rogowski

One of the bright stars of the Black Dirt region is Cheryl Rogowski, 55, who in 2004 was a winner of the McArthur "Genius" Award, the first and only fulltime farmer to win the distinction. And, like many rock stars, her fortunes took a dramatic dive in 2014 when her entire farm operation was sold from under her for non-payment of taxes. Her financial troubles she directly attributes to the devastation of her farm following the weeks of flooding at harvest time that followed hurricane Irene in 2011, and then the effects of Super-storm Sandy the following year.

The dramatic and public crash of a big farm operation is part of the history of the valley and further proof of the vulnerability of its farmers. Through the summer of 2015 Rogowski was fighting the sale in the New York State Supreme Court, claiming proper notification procedures were not followed when her farm was sold. She filed for Chapter 12 bankruptcy, which is designed for agricultural enterprises. Though the farm no longer belonged to her, while the battle continued in court she kept her farm enterprises running, and reported that some of them, like her unique on-farm barn breakfasts, were doing better than ever.

But in the fall of 2015, Rogowski lost part of the legal battle and was given an eviction notice. The barn was locked and she had to abandon her fields. One of the best known and most enterprising farm operations in the region seemed to have folded.

Not so fast! Rogowski still had a slight legal chance of regaining her farm, she said. "No matter what, it's not the end. It's a new beginning."

Rogowski became known throughout the region and beyond for the same reasons she won the McArthur award – her innovations as a grower, her marketing enterprise, community involvement and a plethora of agri-entrepreneurial projects. She was outstanding not only because of the range of crops she grew, but also how she grew them and the way she marketed them. Perhaps most notable is that she was the only grower who cooked her produce and sold it as meals on the farm. With money she was awarded by the McArthur Foundation ($500,000 over five years) she built a kitchen in the main barn and founded Black Dirt Gourmet, the region's only farm-to-table catering operation – she called it "table-on-farm."

She soon started providing country style weekend breakfasts in her barn, a move that dumfounded some in the farming community for whom a barn is the last place you'd eat a meal. Rogowski had recognized there was charm and appeal in the farm environment for the vast demographic who are now disconnected from "the land." After Ye Jolly Onion Inn closed in 2008, Cheryl started an upscale supper club, seating people at long tables in her barn for six course, often sold-out monthly dinners. They were voted the best country dining experience in Orange County by the readers of the

Times Herald-Record, the major local newspaper.

As a woman farm owner/manager, she was a rarity in the muck lands. Though there are increasing numbers of women farmers in the U.S., the Black Dirt is a more patriarchal world. "Family farms" in the Black Dirt include many women as active farming partners – mothers, sisters, wives and daughters. But Rogowski is different; she runs the Rogowski Farm she inherited with her brother and sister when her father Walter died in 1999.

Rogowski was a typical Pine Island lass, raised amidst the traditions and customs of the local Polish community. She was in the Ladies Auxiliary of the Polish Legion of America Veterans (PLAV) at the age of 16. At the 1983 Onion Harvest Festival she was chosen to be an Onion Harvest Princess. She graduated from Mount Saint Mary College in Newburgh with a Bachelor's Degree in International Studies, and then went to work as an accountant for the Sterling Forest Corporation for 20 years (experience that makes the financial problems of the Rogowski Farm business puzzling.) After work each day she'd head straight out to the fields. She fell in love with the soil and talks about it with poetic passion.

When Rogowski took over the family enterprise her father had already started to move away from wholesale onions to other vegetables, and she followed his lead, experimenting with a range of crops. She eventually was growing about 300 varieties on around 150 acres, 30 of which remained fallow at any given time.

She recalls that innovation was not respected in the Black Dirt farming community until recent times. "There was resistance to change. I took risks. A few years ago I started doing hi-tunnel greenhouses stretching the growing season to year round. Now," she points into the landscape, "they are everywhere."

She described her farming practices as "beyond organic" because she shunned allowable "organic" pesticides, preferring a range of practices such as crop rotation and trap cropping – growing plants that attract insects away from her produce.

Rogowski was one of the first farmers to adopt Community Supported Agriculture (CSA), whereby customers buy a season's produce ahead of the season, and then have it delivered to them weekly. CSA helped to guarantee a supply of fresh produce to consumers, while subsidizing the farmer's growing costs.

In the 1980s, when Black Dirt growers were warily switching from onions to other vegetables, farmers' markets were just getting going in New York City. She soon jumped on the veggie wagon and trucked her produce to eight farmers' markets throughout the city and outer boroughs.

Rogowski also played a leading role in founding the first farmers' market in Warwick - a successful summer Sunday enterprise that draws about 1,000 buyers a week from miles around. She had already started selling her produce in her barn on Glenwood Road, between Pine Island and Vernon, NJ, and in 2010 she started a monthly winter market there. She never tired of finding new ways to bring the public to the farm: walking tours to identify edible weeds, tomato harvest festivals in the summer and concerts in her barn.

As a child Rogowski played with the farm workers and became fluent in Spanish. Her connection to the immigrant worker community is profound. Among those who worked on her farm were three generations of the same family. She supported literacy programs for migrant workers and was an advisor to FARMroots, the Greenmarket Immigrant Farmer Program in New York City, which helps migrant farm workers develop their own farms. "These are people trying to make a life, make a living. They are, after all, in the same position my parents and grandparents were in when they came here," Rogowski says.

A soft-spoken woman with a big laugh she says she is far shyer than her public life and barn hospitality suggest. "I am introverted. Public life is difficult." She is aware of wariness towards her in the Polish farming community because she is a woman. "There's a code of conduct established for a man's world. I don't belong." In the rest of the U.S., the number of farms operated by women has more than doubled since 1978, from just 100,000 to almost 250,000 today, according the United States Department of Agriculture. In 2006 *The New York Times* featured Cheryl Rogowski as one of that growing roster of women farmers who have changed the face of American farming.

She told the Times: "Farming has changed, and farmers have to do things they are traditionally really bad at: marketing, educating consumers, collective action, communication...it can't be coincidence that women are traditionally good at those things. I can do every job on this farm that my dad or brother could – operate the forklift, bag onions, haul manure. The fact is that in modern farming it's not enough to drive a tractor. A large array of skills is required."

Apart from the McArthur "Genius" award, Rogowski has a string of awards and distinctions at County and State level. The Pine Island Chamber of Commerce voted her Citizen of the year in 2008. There were tears in her eyes when she accepted the award. "To me the most important thing," she said, "is being recognized by my own community."

Thanks to many in the community who rallied to her side when she was evicted from the farm, Rogowski rented a patch of Black Dirt farmland off Little York, and immediately started planting. She planned to take down her hi-tunnels in the fields of the old farm and re-assemble them on the new property and would use them to start growing winter produce. "And I've rented a barn," she said, sounding upbeat, "where I'm storing things from the kitchen so when I find a suitable venue I can reopen Black Dirt Gourmet and start doing meals again." Perhaps typical of a farmer who has come through a catastrophic season, she's looking ahead. "Really, I see a new beginning."

Chris and Eve Pawelski

Chris Pawelski, a fourth generation onion farmer, might be the rock singer of the Black Dirt, the man who for 20 years has used his voice, spoken and written, to schmooze, argue, cheer, complain, rage and politically lobby on behalf of farmers in the Black Dirt region, while continuing to plant, weed, fertilize and harvest. With his wife Eve, he has made several trips to DC every year to sing the political songs on behalf of farmers back home.

He's smart, outspoken, and always ready to laugh, though he's been more than $150,000 in debt for years – a situation that only improved after he had an outstanding 2014 harvest. Like many of the Black Dirt farmers, he has been devastated by years of weather disasters and flooding. He's in the same shoes as many of the farmers he represents when he catches the train to Union Station in Washington DC, and then walks the "corridors of power" making their case.

Some of the farmers he fights for are not happy about asking for help from anyone, let alone the Federal Government. Fiercely independent, they wish they didn't need to ask Washington for anything, even when Congress was willing to give billions of dollars in subsidies to the big commodity farmers out west, some of whom are millionaires. But Pawelski knows that nothing in the muddle of laws that inhibit agricultural productivity and threaten the future of the family farms will change unless farmers make their voices heard.

What got Chris and Eve Pawelski going was the old Department of Agriculture crop insurance program rules. They required him and other farmers in the valley to continue to fertilize and spray crops against weeds and bugs, even though the produce was effectively dead, killed by a mid-summer hailstorm just as the plants were bulbing. The farmers wanted to destroy their crops, cut their losses and start anew. He was told no, he'd have to keep feeding and dressing the corpses, at enormous cost, or he would not be eligible for the insurance payout. As though Kafka had written the story, when he did make his claim, the insurance program payout was miniscule. It put him and other growers in the valley deep in debt.

So arcane and inadequate was the specialty crop insurance, it sometimes returned less than the amount that farmers paid in premiums. As a result, many farmers didn't even bother to buy it. Indeed, one year the Pawelski's weather-related loss amounted to $100,000. He received far less than his $10,000 premium payment.

The Pawelski's sang a long, plaintive song. They made repeated trips to Washington for six years as they lobbied for improved insurance and tried to get disaster aid for the losses of 1996 and subsequent years. Eventually, with the help of then Congressman Ben Gilman, there was a $10 million payout to Black Dirt onion farmers devastated by years of hail and flooding attached to the 2002 Farm Bill (whose total value was $270 billion).

The couple's long, unremunerated struggle for this and other changes for the small-farm agricultural sector in the Black Dirt region and beyond is documented in his funny, interesting and often shocking manuscript for his book "*Muckville: Farm Policy, Media and the Strange Oddities of Semi-Rural Life.*" It's a memoir, "an inside look at a farmer's fight to influence ag policy in Washington D.C., and the oddities of life that happen along the way." (He has an agent and expects to have a book publisher soon.)

Pawelski has worked closely with elected officials of both parties on the federal, state and county level. Many of the politicians he has engaged in his fights to get help for farmers have come to the Pawelski family farm off Pulaski Highway where Chris, his father Rich and brother Brian grow onions and a little winter squash on about 100 acres.

It's not just politicians who use the Pawelski's as a resource. A few credits shy of a Ph.D in Communications, he is now considered the go-to regional farmer by electronic and print media around the world. As a media expert with a keen news eye, Pawelski is also good at alerting the Press to issues that need attention – usually flooding or other weather disasters. Reporters home in on the Pawelski farm for reliable sound bites from someone knowledgeable on agricultural issues. As well as the prominent national outlets – *CNN*, *The New York Times*, etc, – Chris and Eve have been cover models for farmers on industry magazines, appeared in *Vogue*, and been interviewed by reporters for the *British Broadcasting Corporation* and the *Hindi Times*.

Pawelski Farms, on Pulaski Highway about three miles from Russ Kowal (Chapter 2) has been in existence for about 100 years, since Chris's great-grandfather Frank arrived from Poland in 1903 and bought a dairy farm. He added onions and eventually sold the milking cows. Chris's grandfather John took it on, growing onions, lettuce and carrots on about 20 acres. John, one of the first farmers to use a "riding tractor" in the muck lands, began to focus on onions, which was the sole crop when Chris's father Richard took over. Like many farms, the acreage increased over the years to keep up with growing costs. As onions prices remained static those farmers who could not expand went out of business.

Chris was helping his father pack onions in crates at the age of five and was muscling the wheel of farm vehicles when he was 11. A Pine Islander who taught him at high school said his future was predictable: he was outgoing and smart. He graduated from the State University of New York (SUNY) at Cortland and moved west to get his Masters in Broadcasting and Film Studies at the University of Iowa where he met Eve, also a student of communications. He taught courses for a few years, and spent a few more in the corporate world.

"But I started to yearn to be back on the farm. The pull of the farm won." In 1993 he and Eve left the Midwest for Pine Island, moved into the small house on the farm, once inhabited by his grandparents, and became onion farmers.

It was the hail of 1996 that pushed them into debt – and provoked them to become activists for changes in farm policy. Since then, Chris and Eve Pawelski have fought government politicians and officials at one level or another on almost every issue that confounds and threatens the survival of the farmers. The one exception is the weather – and they would probably take that on too if they had access to divine power.

He has proposed a change to the agricultural labor section of the immigration bill that would make the unpopular H-2A visa for foreign farm workers simpler, less confusing and more efficient. And at State level he has lobbied ferociously against sections of the Farm Workers Fair Labor Practices Bill that would initiate overtime pay, and allow collective bargaining (among other provisions), which he says would make small farming in New York State uneconomical and put farms out of business.

For years Pawelski has argued for federal funds to be spent to help prevent another catastrophic flood by the Wallkill River. He has improved the onion crop loss insurance program for Black Dirt farmers, and devised a new $50 million Conservation on Muck Soils program (COMS). The House version passed in 2008, but not the Senate version. It would prevent soil erosion and protect water quality on the banks of the rivers, through a program that allows voluntary retirement and cover-cropping of farm land.

"I have tried to convince the local farmers that if they don't talk to the press the other's guy's viewpoint will be accepted. You've got to get your side of the story out." More importantly, he says, "when there's a problem you have to argue it and then present a solution." It is a philosophy that has earned him praise across the political spectrum: some of those solutions have been adopted as legislation and more are sure to follow.

He makes not a penny from the media and lobbying for farmers and relies on his wife to help support the family from her job as an assistant librarian at the nearby Chester School District. His home on Pulaski Highway is small considering the power and celebrity he wields in the world of political power. Although he is controversial, and some farmers shy away from him (even though they might benefit from his lobbying efforts), there's not one other farmer in the entire region with both the political and the media clout of this onion farmer.

One Saturday while he was grading and packing red onions in his barn, Eve sat in their living room with their two boys, Caleb and Jonah, folding the family laundry. Eve was asked about the future – would her boys go into farming?

"I hope not!" she says, immediately. But then after a pause she adds: "Look, there are some great things about it. The boys have their Dad here at all times. It's great if they get sick or need something." Caleb speaks up: "My Dad is always just out there..." he points to the barn and the Black Dirt fields. Now, Caleb, who is 19, enjoys working on the farm and already looks like a future farmer. But Eve and Chris are insistent on one thing. Both boys must get a college degree before they even decide whether or not to become farmers.

Recently, Pawelski started a professional lobby group called Farmroot, a non-profit that advocates on behalf of America's specialty crop family farms and includes experts in the issues that affect them – a reliable, legal farm work force with an appropriate safety net, funding for scientific research specific to specialty crops, and access to affordable and reliable crop insurance.

Farmroot is also spearheading a proposal for a program to enable specialty crop farmers to directly supply food to food banks, food pantries and food recovery programs – connecting farmers with the "food insecure," and by-passing repackers and terminal markets. Eventually, Pawelski hopes, Farmroot will enable him to earn something from the lobbying work that he has been doing as a volunteer on behalf of the farming community for more than 20 years.

Alex Paffenroth

The top chefs on the East Coast – call them the glitterati of the gourmet world – adore Alex Paffenroth, the Black Dirt produce farmer whose stand at the Union Square Market has become a foodie destination.

Famous names like Dan Barber of Blue Hill at Stone Barns and Dan Kluger ("Best New Chef 2012") of ABC Kitchen go to him for exotic, unusual or even slightly sensational crops that makes their dishes truly cutting edge.

The chefs at some of the top rated restaurants in New York, eateries including Gramercy Tavern, Eleven Madison Park, Telepan, Union Square Café, WD 50, Cookshop – and about 30 more - frequent the Paffennroth Gardens farm stand on the Northwest Corner of Union Square on Wednesdays and Saturdays.

Known as "the Root King" in New York's foodie world, he sells about 24 varieties of root crops. They are just some of the 200 varieties grown at Paffenroth Gardens off Little York Road. There are 20 varieties of potatoes alone. Paffenroth's range of multi-colored carrots – purple, yellow, white and red – are so stunning they caught the attention of Martha Stewart, who came to the Black Dirt to do a photo shoot.

"I have experimented with many things – like burdock, salsify, scorzonera (a black salsify that the French love) and even dandelion root. That was very bitter. Some things fly, some don't. This spring I tried mache, a delicate lettuce – it's like spinach. You can harvest it even when there's still snow on the ground. New York chefs love what's new and different."

Early one spring morning Alex Paffenroth was working in his office. It's part of the farmhouse, which is set below Little York Road on the slopes of Mount Eve, and looks out over Paffenroth Gardens' Black Dirt fields and a large blue barn. Nailed to the wall are about a dozen Zagat reviews, all tributes to the range and freshness of his Union Square market vegetables, and they note how inexpensive is his produce.

He was perusing a vegetable catalogue called Johnny's Selected Seeds, a compendium of the latest varieties and an important resource for produce farmers – those growing staples as well as the green market crowd looking for the exciting and off-beat. Before he heads to Manhattan he uses his computer to broadcast to his list of about 40 restaurants the novel greens he will be selling next day – a smart move that's typical of how farmers are using internet technology to help their businesses.

His savvy and success in New York must be seen in the context of recent Black Dirt history. A few decades ago Alex Paffentroth was nearly wiped out. He hung on by a root tendril.

In 1987 when he was an onion soloist like his father, his crop was annihilated by hail. "Fifty acres, gone. I lost pretty much everything. Almost gave up. I was left farming just 12 acres. Then I was hit by hail again the following year.

"I was trying to sell the farm. But I had two daughters to support. My wife Linda had started doing some green market sales, but I was never too interested in that. I'd always sold wholesale. Anyway, I started to get into the green market business, going down with a pickup, at first to Middletown and New Jersey. I thought, you could never make enough money from this. But I had no alternative. And then business grew.

"I applied to get into the Wednesday market in Union Square in New York, and in about 1990 I was accepted. First, I was small scale, selling basic items - radishes, onions, herbs. Then I learned about what people wanted – things like arugula that we'd never heard of out here. So I started looking for things that were new."

In his effort to supply city customers with the novel and the off-beat, Paffenroth expanded his farm to over 200 vegetable varieties. Word of his specialties spread and with his popularity came an opening to be at Union Square on Saturdays as well. Now, all year round two truckloads make the Saturday run to Union Square, where Linda Paffenroth manages the stand. On Wednesdays, from June to Christmas, Alex takes the produce to the market and runs the operation with his daughter Deanne, a physical therapist who helps to set up in the morning. She has a doctorate in physical therapy and leaves the stand to do her evaluation of pre-school children to determine their need for treatment. She lives with her husband and two children nearby in Warwick.

Deanne was at the register in Union Square one day when she was asked about a slightly succulent green on sale – it resembled a persistent weed that people remove from their garden every year. "It's purslane," she nods. "A weed to most people. But it's also great raw in salads. It's like watercress or spinach. You can also cook it – steamed or stir fried." Purslane was Paffenroth Gardens' special of the day.

Although Deanne helps out, she doesn't want to farm. "As a physiotherapist she makes more in a day than I make in a week," says her father. As in many Black Dirt farm families, a second income helps the Paffenroth Gardens enterprise. "My wife's salary makes it all possible," says Paffenroth. She has a job in human resources at Amscan, a company that makes party and paper goods in nearby Chester, NY. And their daughter Amanda helps on the farm and keeps the homestead running while her parents are at work. She adores cats, which abound in the house and the farm.

Unlike many other Black Dirt farmers who circulate among the farmers' markets throughout the tristate region from day to day, the Paffenroth family is dedicated to the Union Square market. The gig requires a 3 AM rise in order to cover the 90-minute drive to 14th Street, and then time needed to set up the tables. Over their stand they erect a large orange Paffenroth Gardens canopy that casts such a distinctive color over the huge array of produce it all appears to lie in a sunset glow.

Alex Paffenroth is a third generation farmer of Volga German heritage, whose ancestors settled in the Little York region in 1850s. He grew up on this land, helping his dad. "My father wanted me to farm with him, but I wasn't interested and signed up to join the army. It was the stupidest thing I ever did. My father died just as I was heading off to Vietnam. I got a compassionate discharge and came back to run the farm for a year, and then another year. And another.

"I think you almost have to grow up in it to do it. It's hard, hard work, and long hours. Why we do it is actually a mystery."

Among the problems he names is acquiring labor for the fields. "The general public doesn't understand the problems farmers have with labor. Vegetable farmers need seasonal workers – we don't need people year round. I wake up in the morning and wonder if I'm going to have workers to help that day."

An amiable, soft-spoken man, he insists he's not complaining about his life. "I enjoy everything I do. Whatever I do I make sure I enjoy it. You have a choice: you can be happy or sad. I made my choice. We farmers become philosophical – you have to be. There's so much that's out of your control, including the weather, and the way prices go up and down."

And, of course, getting older. He's 70, with grayish hair. He says he's slowing down, and becoming a little hard of hearing. Eventually he won't be able to farm. And since neither of his daughters want to take over Paffenroth Gardens, he doesn't know what will happen to the farming operation.

"But I want to stay right here in the house we built, looking out over the fields." He looks up through the window to the farm and the bright blue barns with their menagerie of cats – 17 of them. "That view holds such memories for me. "I'm not going anywhere. After all," he adds with a smile, "my roots are here!"

Leonard and Valorie DeBuck

One late winter morning Leonard DeBuck was driving his large white truck around the perimeter of his 360-acre farm on the Mission Land tract. The Wallkill River zigzagged beside the farm road, a murky brown waterway that flows through the plain and occasionally causes terrible damage. The remnants of a light snowfall were whipped by the wind across the monotone landscape – such a colorless contrast with the emerald of these fields in the summer. Leonard stopped beside a large field, defined by eight feet deep drainage ditches. "Here is the soul of my farm. Right here," he says, looking to the east where the low upland ridge, the Pochuck Neck, is scattered with the farmsteads and warehouses that border the Mission Land.

Though he's been here for 30 years, Lenny, as he is called by many of his friends in the valley, is a relative newcomer to the Black Dirt Region, a "transplant" he'd be called. He moved east from Michigan in 1980, straight out of Michigan State University, where he had just graduated with a degree in agronomy. The youngest of eight children, he and his four brothers all went into sod farming, following in their father Leo's footsteps. Lenny had done a summer internship in the Black Dirt and so when the Gurda farm was foreclosed and vast acreage became available, he bought a tract of Black Dirt and moved east.

The young DeBuck was accompanied by his new wife Valorie, his high school sweetheart. She had just earned a degree in accounting and has done the books for the DeBuck farm enterprises since day one. They moved into a two-bedroom trailer home on French's Island, one of the serene uplands rising out of their Mission Land Black Dirt farmland. After seven years they built their own house on the island, where they live today.

An agri-entrepreneur brimming with new ideas, Lenny diversified in 1990, building a golf practice range on his sod farm. Four year's later he upgraded it to the 9-hole Scenic Farms Golf Course. Lenny has also expanded his crops to include some fields of corn and soybeans. But perhaps his greatest innovation is earth-friendly sod farming practices – relevant in a time when growing and maintaining turf lawns is frequently vilified as environmentally poisonous – especially by purveyors of astro-turf and other man-made green ground covers.

"People think farmers use a lot of chemicals. What I use is best management practices. I use less than other people because I try to work closely with Mother Nature, so she does the work for me. It's simply understanding the change of the seasons. I won't broadcast grass seed in the spring because I have 90 days of summer ahead, when my seeds are competing with all those other weed seeds. I want to plant my seeds on the hottest day of the year – in the middle of August when the other seeds have already germinated. Then three or four weeks later guess who comes to call? Jack Frost. He kills almost every weed and never sends a bill. Free! If there are a few perennial weeds around – dandelions among them – I eradicate them with a specific herbicide.

"The lawn that goes into winter as an adolescent becomes a mature adult by June, so that the sunlight, the essence of germination, won't penetrate the grass and reach the soil and the weeds trying to grow beneath. So I don't do a dime of crabgrass prevention or eradication. I'm convinced I spend less on chemicals than the average domestic lawn grower."

Lenny is a poetic man, known to recite a poem at a Town Council meeting to make a point, and like all farmers, he's philosophical. However, like so many growers in the fertile Black Dirt region, he is a little cynical about those consumers who are proponents of a strict organic food system. "They are the same people who go to supermarkets and shop with their eyes, intolerant of blemishes or specks, the slight imperfections that come with organic farming. The same people who sit in a car in New York inhaling toxic fumes!"

DeBuck's Sod Farm predominantly grows Kentucky Blue Grass because it is premium quality with the much desired green-blue hue, and a rhizomatous root system. Underground, the mother plant sends up daughter plants, spreading via the root system, he explains. "Economically, I can grow the rich, Cadillac lawn at the same price as the Chevrolet lawn. It is partly our rich soil. But it takes 21 days to germinate. That's longer than most homeowners can wait because other weeds will take over in that amount of time.

"I also do some fine Fescue grass, which can grow in partial shade. It's all good for athletic fields, corporate headquarters, everything that needs grass." Along with five other turf grass growers, Lenny estimates there are between 1,800 and 2,400 acres of Black Dirt nurturing sod when the economy is strong. But sod is a highly specialized crop, requiring expert species knowledge, specialized machinery, and very particular marketing, selling and delivery/collection systems and equipment. Because turf grass is so vulnerable to poor economic climates he, like the other Black Dirt sod farmers, recently converted some of his acreage to other crops, mainly soybeans.

Having suffered severe losses from flooding of the Wallkill River over the past decades, Lenny is deeply involved in efforts to improve the flow of the river that borders his farm. The question is who pays? "We have a Department of Transport that takes care of roads when they deteriorate. They fix the potholes. We are not asking for bigger or better, just a department that deals with the water. New York State and the Federal Government should share responsibility."

Lenny served on the Warwick Town Board for 14 years, until 2012, fulfilling an injunction from his father that he serve the community. The early years as a farmer/elected official were tough. "When you run your own farm, you call the shots. When you are one of a board of five in a town the size of Warwick, things move much more slowly. It takes time for ideas to spread and grow after they are planted. Often it takes even more time to convince people your idea is a good one."

Warwick was going through a major zoning overhaul during his first years in office. There were 250 meetings over ten years dealing with issues related to farmland use. The growing problem was that as more people moved to live in Warwick, more open land was being lost to development. Action was needed to retain the rural character of the town and keep farmland – what Lenny calls "a working landscape." Under his leadership Warwick took three measures:

- Introduced the Purchase of Developments Rights, so farmers could get equity out of their property without selling to developers and land would stay in agriculture.
- Changed the zoning laws to give incentives for developers and their design engineers to cluster new homes in one area and leave large areas, green space, open for conservation instead of dividing a lot into large plots.
- Loosened the restrictions on what buildings farmers could put up to enable them to become more profitable, and more likely to stay in farming. (Hence, a dairy farmer was able to build an ice cream retail outlet.)

"Some farmers believed that what we were planning would destroy the equity they had in their land. I was reviled. It was really ugly," Lenny recalls. However, he believed in what he was promoting for the region. The eventual zoning changes preserved farmland and helped farmers retain land value. Many farmers, who initially opposed the plans, took advantage of the new zoning. The Warwick changes not only helped retain the rural charm of the region, the program won statewide awards and has been duplicated in many other regions.

He has been an active advocate for farmers on other issues: He opposed the federal plan to expand a wetland preserve for wildlife into the Black Dirt farmland. "It has no place here," he says. "Why expand here where you have people growing food, feeding families and making a payroll?"

Many decisions related to the DeBuck sod farm are now made by his eldest son Greg, 32, who is one of the young farmers taking over the family farm from their parents. Lenny has for 25 years served on the board of the Pine Island Chamber of Commerce, where he currently is president. It was Lenny who spearheaded the move to plant trees in the heart of the hamlet, bringing gentle splashes of green to that swathe of blacktop grey, and he spread spring wildflower seeds along the roadsides.

He was asked what were the biggest misconceptions about farmers. "One is about sustainability. Farmers don't work the land as though it's something to be disposed of in two years. They invest in it, to leave it in better shape. They are good stewards of the land and the environment around them. Otherwise they couldn't survive."

Another outdated misconception, he says, is what and who farmers are – that those who farm were unable to get a university degree or do a higher-paying, professional job off the farm. "The majority of farmers now have college degrees, and some have advanced degrees." He thinks "agricultural engineer" is an appropriate term for farmers of today.

Bob and Sally Scheuermann

Visitors are often delighted by the charm of Little York. There can be few more delightfully unpretentious country settlements on the East Coast than this upland where Volga Germans arrived in the 1700s. The scene is a white Lutheran church with its elegant steeple, and small clapboard houses nestling along Mount Eve, all facing out over neatly delineated fields. This is where the ancestors of produce and flower farmer Bob Scheuermann bought a small plot in the 1730s.

Scheuermanns are still scattered around the region, including their son Rob, who runs a landscaping business. Other fourth and fifth generation descendents of Volga Germans still live in the settlement. Now however, only half the Little York residents are of German descent. The few who are still farming have gradually bought farms from those leaving agriculture, greatly increasing the size of their farms from a few acres to anything from 35 to 80 acres. "Many of our fields are named for the people we bought them from," says Bob's wife, Sally. "The Daubert Ground, the Sudol Fields, the Paffenroth Fields…"

The Scheuermann's state-certified nursery is a vivid splash of country color. In planting season they maintain over 2,000 pots of perennial flowers and a wide variety of annuals and vegetable bedding plants, hanging baskets, patio pots, and nursery stock. Apart from five greenhouses, the Scheuermann's grow 35 acres of produce, most famously tomatoes, sweet corn, potatoes and beans, which they sell to about a dozen area restaurants.

The distinctive thing about Bob and Sally is that, unlike most muck land farmers who sell their produce off site, the Scheuermann's go to great lengths to entice customers to their landscaped Black Dirt farm. "My thing," says Bob, "is to bring people here. When people come to the farm they want to go out and actually feel the black soil in their fingers. We make it possible to walk about and see what we love about this place."

Their particular ways of bringing people onsite include hosting public music concerts, as part of the Warwick Arts Festival. For the past 14 years, thousands of people have spread out on the lawn beside their farm fields, listening to music as the sun goes down over the Black Dirt.

For the past six summers they have hosted the Pine Island Chamber of Commerce's annual Black Dirt Feast, a fabulously successful six course (always sold out) dinner for more than 200 people, served Tuscan style out in the fields. Perhaps the most heralded foodie event in the Black Dirt, it is a celebration of the produce of the region and its chefs who serve one of the six courses.

A high proportion of the Scheuermanns' business is in greenhouses so the Scheuermann's have a small measure of protection from one of those elements that threaten other Black Dirt farmers – the weather. "But one year I lost my entire onion crop to three minutes of hail," recalls Bob. "We keep going because we always believe next year's crop will be better. Philosophically, we farmers have to be optimists."

Like many farmers, the Scheuermanns believe that the Federal Government has abandoned the Black Dirt farmers. "They couldn't care less about Orange County. They'd rather forget about us. The Wallkill River hasn't been dredged in 40 years. And efforts to get compensation after Hurricane Irene went nowhere. We got low interest loans. That's All! Nothing will happen unless, perhaps, it's an election year."

They both note that while the Federal Government will not help existing Black Dirt farmers, it is providing financial assistance to new farmers through a program to help minorities get into agriculture. "Creating competition for those farmers already struggling, who they refuse to help!"

Like other farmers, the Scheuermanns said the failure of Washington to fix the immigration laws made it so difficult for migrant farm workers to come and go legally that labor was becoming increasingly difficult to obtain. "Adding insult to injury, the Federal Government insists every year that we fill in a survey, pages of details about what we farm. It takes a long time. But we get no acknowledgment and never hear any report on what they learn from these surveys," said Bob, repeating a complaint made by sod farmer Leonard DeBuck. "Yet when we need help, we don't exist.

"The shame is that farmers don't want handouts, we live modestly, and like being independent. When we make money we put it straight back into the land or new equipment."

A handsome and devoted couple, they met when Sally Laroe was 18 and Bob was 19. Her family, an exotic mix of French, Dutch and German, had been farmers in Sugar Loaf, NY, ten miles away, for five generations. Bob, who was strictly an onion farmer like his forebears, knew that eventually he would have to diversity.

He gives Sally credit for the start of their flourishing horticulture and greenhouse business. "Sally loves flowers and when I saw how much she was spending on them I thought, lets grow our own!" What started out as one 2,500 square foot greenhouse has become a 10,000 sq foot greenhouse and nursery business.

Scheuermann Farms includes a store, whimsically named "Ooops I Forgot Gift Shop," where Sally also sells gifts and garden and patio supplies, including decorative stepping stones and glass birdbaths. And every year they introduce new varieties of flowers and vegetables to their greenhouse business.

They also provide a "Bring Your Own Planter" service, whereby customers bring their deck box to the greenhouses, fill their container with soil mix and pick out the exact plants they want, with Bob and Sally on hand for advice. Some customers leave the container for Sally, who studied art and has a creative flair, to fill for them.

The Scheuermanns have lived at their farm on Little York Road for 45 years and plan to be there for a good many more. "We say there is no prettier place than where we live. and the sunsets are spectacular. We want people to come out here and see what we see, see what we love doing," says Sally. "You have to really love doing this," adds Bob, "Because no one here goes into farming for the money."

Vinny and Denise D'Attolico

Vinny D'Attolico is certainly not the only Black Dirt farmer of Italian heritage. But his family was the first in the muck lands to go completely organic. With his wife Denise he cultivates six acres at the southernmost tip of the Mission Land tract. "We are purists," he says. "And one of the very few farmers in the valley who are certified."

He took over from his mother and father, Vince and Joan D'Attolico, who were popular vendors at the Union Square greenmarket in Manhattan in its early days. They were among just a handful of farmers supplying organically grown produce. (His father died in 1997.)

"My Dad was one of nine children, but the only one born here. The others all came from Italy via Ellis Island. They grew up on a homestead farm on Long Island where my father's mom taught him everything about food and vegetables and crops."

Vincent D'Attolico Sr. had been an electrical engineer and doing well until the recession in the early 1970s. He moved his family to the Greenwood Lake area, where he started to garden. "As a kid, my job was to pick out the rocks, which I hated," recalls Vinny. "Then in 1976 when I was 13 we moved here, to the Black Dirt. And I hated it even more. I missed the lake and our boat, and I didn't know anyone here."

Vinny confesses that he was stubborn as a young man. "I did this and that, and eventually went into the Armed Forces. I served in Germany for four years, which I enjoyed. It was part of a 'walkabout' that ends where you are meant to be, philosophically, if not geographically."

One night in 1990, shortly after his return home from Germany, he stopped at the Sundowner, one of the many pubs in Pine Island in those days. Denise Decker, who had grown up in Warwick, was sitting at the bar. "I knew then. We loved each other from the start. We are friends. We talk about everything and work together 24/7. We knew we'd be together forever," says Vinny. They married in 2003 and have a nine-year-old daughter.

The D'Attolico farm is owned by Vinny's mother Joan, with whom he is close. He has three sisters, none of whom farms the family plot.

Vinny and Denise laugh a lot, even though being an organic purist in the Black Dirt, where weeds thrive, can be financially challenging and very frustrating. "We see the vegetables grown by conventional farming methods maturing three times faster because of the fertilizers and pesticides. Onion farmers put chemicals on their crops nine times each growing season, and they have to wear protective gear. Why eat the food?" asks Vinny, wryly.

Then he's contrite. "Look, its hard to bad mouth them," he said. "Its how they farm."

The D'Attolico's have a handful of greenhouses where they grow mache, arugula, wheatgrass, bean sprouts and other winter crops. They are dedicated to chemical free farming and willingly pay the $875 it costs each year for all the paperwork and processing involved in becoming officially certified as organic farmers. (About 75% of that cost is reimbursed.) The process involves inspections – some unannounced – that take place through the year. They happily live with the required fallow 50-foot buffer zone between their farm fields and their non-organic farm neighbors so that no chemicals can drift onto their crops.

In their fields on a fall day they bent over picking kale and carrots for the greenmarket in New York's Union Square. The fields were filled with low growing weeds, which thrive in the Black Dirt. They said the weeds would help protect their crops from the frost. When weeds are out of control they get rid of them with a roto-tiller. Denise picked some mustard greens as evidence that organically grown food is tastier. (It was fiercely mustardy.)

Vinny said customers often return to their farm market stand to compliment them on their produce's superior taste. "You don't get the same flavor if you rush the growth with fertilizers. Ours grow and fill out at their own pace."

Many people eat organically grown food not just because they want their produce without what they believe to be dangerous chemicals, but also because they are ill and prefer to try a healthy diet rather than start chemotherapy. The D'Attolicos believe firmly in the healing power of healthy food. Vinny quotes Hippocrates, the founder of modern medicine: "Let food be your medicine. Let medicine be your food." They have dedicated considerable time to experimentation with a variety of sprouted seeds which are believed to have valuable qualities for human health.

Even if their produce doubles as both food and medicine, the D'Attolico's said they do not charge markedly more for their produce than conventional growers, and sometimes charge less. The challenges are greater and the yields lower and it often takes longer to grow their crops, which Vinny says is all fine. It is clear that at this point Vinny and Denise's biggest rewards are existential, not financial. Since 2002 Vinny has had a winter job delivering fuel to help pay the bills in the cold months. However, even the financial aspects are better than they were a few years ago.

After Hurricane Irene in 2011 and the flooding of the Wallkill River that courses through the Black Dirt about a mile away from their smallholding, their crops were submerged under several feet of water for weeks.

"Everything was ready for harvesting - tomatoes, cayenne peppers, string beans. It was skid row for us. People said FEMA (Federal Emergency Management Agency) might help but they only do residential and commercial loss, not agricultural."

Vinny shrugs. "We didn't lose our lives, or our house, or the land. We saw what happened to other people who lost everything. Who are we to complain?"

They both commented with gratitude on the Farm Aid fundraising effort organized by the people of Warwick after the disastrous flooding. "About $100,000 was divided among 45 farmers. The money, about $2,175, helped us pay our bills. People would come up to us and say here's $100. Save it for next year."

With a few zero-interest credit cards they bought seeds for the next season. They gradually replaced the greenhouses that had been shredded by Irene, and started again.

But the next spring saw The Invasion of the Crop Predators. There were deer, groundhogs and rabbits, all of which have a voracious appetite for tender saplings. Deer devoured 3,200 feet of baby carrots. "I bought electric fencing, but while the batteries were charging I had to stand watch in the field all night, yelling at them to go away.

"Here's how you define farmer rage," says Vinny. "Its when you walk into your field in the morning and the woodchucks have eaten 100 yards of beans. They've had a helluva party and left their beer cans and sun screen...." It wouldn't occur to him to shoot the woodchucks, as the law allows. Nor the rabbits, raccoons, and deer that all abound in the Wildlife Refuge close by and that prey on their crops.

The Black Dirt farming community is filled with devoted couples who work together as business partners like Denise and Vinny. "On all issues, we talk things out," says Vinny. "Sometimes she'll say 'its time to pull the carrots, and I'll say no, give them another few days. They are more tender when they are younger, but they are bigger when they're in the ground longer, and fetch a little more."

"But sometimes we have to pull them anyway," shrugs Denise, "because we need the money." ■

PART TWO:
THE PROBLEMS

CHAPTER SIX: WEATHER AND WATER
The Boss: Bountiful and Brutal
".....farming here is an important industry benefiting millions of people. Something must be done."

The farmers' only boss is Mother Nature and how generous and full of sweet surprises she can be. Ask about the unexpected delights of 2014 – a gentle spring and sun-filled summer. But she can also be capricious, cruel, and totally indiscriminate. Anyone else in the workforce with a "superior" as ruthless as this one might lodge a complaint with a regulatory agency, try to sue, or simply walk off the job. The latter is the only one of those options available to farmers. If they choose to continue farming they must develop a hardy resilience: deal with it and move on to the next season.

Mother Nature seems to have been particularly harsh on the Black Dirt valley; weather catastrophes have struck with increasing frequency in the past 50 years, seeming to single out these fertile fields with devastating hail, destructive winds, and scorching heat. Then there's the rain. The muck lands and the rivers that run through it – the Wallkill River and its many creeks, which once helped make the soil so fertile – have flooded repeatedly and catastrophically in recent years. The Wallkill basin has flooded following rainfall that only ten years ago would have simply left crops soggy but harvestable. Now, the river overflows, the water does not run off the land and the uplands become islands, where residents make wry comments about their new "lakefront property," though the joke has worn thin.

Maire Ullrich at the CCE explains that for farmers the important climate change is not the temperature as much as it is the rainfall. "The old rain pattern of one inch of rain a week has turned to three inches every three weeks. The intensity of the rain, and the time in between the rainfall has increased."

To the extent that these changes to the climate are a result of human activity they can be slowed or stopped only by worldwide collaboration, including measures taken on farms, large and small, animal and crop. "We cannot fix it all here. What we can do is find ways to survive the changes taking place. Turn lemons into lemonade," says Ullrich. "We must adjust our farming practices to suit new weather patterns - grow different crops better suited to the new conditions."

The worst weather event in recent times was in August 2011, when Hurricane Irene dropped seven inches of rain followed about a week later by Tropical Storm Lee, which added a five inch downpour. As a result the Pochuck Creek and Wallkill Rivers flooded the valley just as produce, ripe for one of the most bountiful harvests in years, lay in the fields.

Floodwaters turned the Black Dirt into the Black Sea. Water rushed at such depth over County Route One it became impassable, isolating Merritts Island in the Mission Land. The fast flowing water flushed thousands of pounds of Paul and John Ruskiewicz's perfectly mature golden onions across the highway into the deep water that was, just the day before, new farmer Tony Bracco's squash fields.

Water was so high in the fields they were navigable by boat. A motorist who underestimated the velocity of the floodwaters over County Route One was swept right off the highway and into a submerged onion field. Paul Kulik, a resident on Merritts Island, heard her screams for help as her car sank in eight feet of water. He dragged out a small boat he stowed in his barn and rowed to the car, saving the life of the driver, who could not swim.

A week later, as water was beginning to recede, rain from Tropical Storm Lee poured down on the region, and exacerbated the flooding.

Several farmers raced the rising flood. Jeff and Adina Bialis on Indiana Road recall watching the water rise as they scrambled to get to harvest the crops before they were submerged. As a result of the new rainfall, produce and sod in some areas lay under water for two weeks and longer. Nothing could survive. Because of the danger of contamination from leaking sewage, petroleum and other contaminants, farmers were told not to harvest crops for market but to abandon them in the fields. The scene was apocalyptic. The smell of rotting produce and heartbreaking loss drenched the valley through the fall.

Cornell Cooperative Extension has estimated $50 million in crops were destroyed in Orange County, much of it in the Black Dirt where the storms wiped out the entire year's harvest on most of the 50-plus family farms, annihilating in one shot the annual income for all those whose crops are garnered at the end of summer. A few farmers were left with hundreds of thousands of dollars in debt, some of it carried over from recent bad years.

It's the nature of the farming business in this region that it is highly dependent on loans to cover expenses for costly fertilizers, pesticides and labor – costs that build up over the year in anticipation of the big annual payout when the crops are sold. An entire crop wiped out at harvest can be financially devastating.

Rain is not the only weather threat. Winds wreak havoc with newly planted seeds, and a few minutes of hail can kill an entire crop at any stage in the growth cycle. Droughts have also become more common, slowing growth and damaging plants. Crop insurance – aka "risk management" – would be the rational solution to keep small farmers from going under when a weather disaster strikes. Indeed, a Federal Crop Insurance Program does exist, with premiums paid by taxpayers. But it is extremely slow to pay out, and what payments farmers receive are considered minimal. Farmers could buy extra insurance through the Supplemental Revenue Assistance Payments Program, but that too is considered inadequate, and unable to deliver immediate assistance. So paltry is the return on the dollar that many farmers didn't bother to buy it.

Because of the higher risks of single crop farming most growers in the Black Dirt have now diversified. Some farmers grow more than two hundred different vegetable and herb varieties on their land. But getting insurance for diversified vegetable farms has been a nightmare.

Crop Insurance has rescued large-scale mono-crop farmers from weather disasters in the United States many times in the past. It was created during the New Deal for the "row" crops of the Midwest – corn, soybeans, wheat, rice and cotton – at a time when they were small and desperately needed help to survive. But they merged and grew over the past 65 years, becoming vast corporate farm co-ops with well financed lobbies in Washington DC that keep the payouts coming. These have been the main beneficiaries of crop insurance, certainly not the small specialty crop farmers of the Northeast. Indeed, during the droughts that devastated the Midwest and Southern states in 2013, payouts were huge and swift. The federal insurance payout for Black Dirt farmers, who lost $50 million due to the catastrophic flooding following Hurricane Irene in 2011, was $5.6m with $720,000 for uninsured farmers.

The new Farm Bill, signed by President Barak Obama in January 2014, promised to bring new, effective crop insurance for small specialty farms. This bill directed the USDA to develop and implement a new whole-farm multiple-crop insurance policy for small crop farmers like those in the Black Dirt. But for Jeff and Adina Bialis of J & A Farm, who grow more than 300 varieties of vegetables and herbs on about 12 acres off Indiana Road, the complicated and detailed record keeping requirements are still so time consuming they decided they'd be better off using their hours actually farming. Their "insurance" is to stagger throughout the growing season a wide range of crops so that the wipeout of one or two varieties would never be crippling.

With insurance or without, for many farmers in the Black Dirt region the changing weather patterns have meant that to continue to farm they have had to abandon some of the crops their parents and grandparents raised, eschewing several generations of agricultural know-how, and learn how to grow different produce, using new methods, fertilizers, pesticides and ground covers. Like a factory suddenly manufacturing a different product, the material, machinery, skills and marketing are different – sometimes radically different. But many farmers in the region have done just that, switching to a variety of new crops that are harvested serially, not all at once, or that are less sensitive to periods of high moisture and drought. As a result, the Black Dirt region is producing a large and growing range of produce with different harvesting timetables.

Frogs vs. Farmers?

But different crops and new agricultural practices will do nothing to overcome the other massive threat to farming in the Black Dirt, one that is often connected to the new rainfall patterns: the flooding of the Black Dirt basin. The increasingly frequent overflowing of the Wallkill River is possibly the biggest threat to farmers in the muck lands and the millions of dollars worth of produce they raise for the tristate region. Unlike the new rainfall patterns, the flooding is something that local farmers, landowners, public officials and fresh food advocates can try to do something about. The issue is what, will there be consensus, and who will pay?

The maverick Wallkill River is a waterway that flows northward, unlike most rivers in the United States that head south. It runs 88 miles from Sussex County, New Jersey, through Orange and Ulster Counties in New York before it slips into the Hudson River at Kingston, New York.

Originally called the Twischsawkin River by Native Americans, it became known as the Palse River by early Dutch settlers in the New Paltz region. It soon became clear that the Palse River extended much further West and South than the town of New Paltz and the Hudson River, so it was renamed the Waal, after a major river in the Netherlands, and kill, the Dutch for river.

A ten mile portion of the Wallkill winds through the Black Dirt farmlands like a tangled ribbon. The river enters the muck lands near the New Jersey border and exits downstream at Denton, near the Wallkill Town line. Normally just a murky but rather benevolent waterway, it lends the Black Dirt valley some charms – the bubbling and gurgling sound where the water courses over rocks, riparian wildlife, a little recreational fishing, and even occasional rafting in the spring. But with water levels many feet below the banks for most of the year, rafting through this region is often a viewless venture, more like a paddle down a deep ditch than through bucolic countryside.

When European settlers arrived in the Wallkill River valley in the 1700s the region was a shallow lake for eight months of the year, the flow of water out of the valley impeded by an accumulation of dense rocks and boulders at the hamlet of Denton (once appropriately known as Outlet), where the Wallkill River exits the muck lands. From the 1770s landowners made repeated attempts to lower the level of the lake by removing these rocks, with limited success.

Over a stretch of two miles beyond the rocky outcrop at Denton the riverbed drops about 24 feet. This led local landowners at the next town,

Hampton, to build a mill to trap hydro-power to operate factories.

Fierce animosity between the upstream landowners and downstream factory owners came to a head after 1826 when New York State gave permission for the farmers upstream to build a three-mile canal to divert the river between Denton, with its rocky outcrops, and Hampton, downstream. With their mill operations threatened, the downstream factory owners tried to stop construction of this new channel.

Named the Cheechunk for a local Indian settlement, the canal was completed in 1835. Its banks soon began to erode and the channel widened. Then a massive storm caused it to overflow. The banks were washed away and the 12-foot wide ditch became a river hundreds of feet wide in parts. It diverted water from the original river and, along with drainage ditches built earlier by the farmers, served effectively to help remove the surface water and do what the farmers had dreamed of; it helped to turn thousands of acres of swamp into fertile farmland which they promptly began to cultivate.

In his *History of Sussex and Warren Counties, NJ*, written in 1881, James P. Snell explains how the desperate downstream factory owners built a dam across the canal to divert the waters back to their original river course, with the effect of flooding the reclaimed farmlands. The farmers ganged up and destroyed the dam. It was rebuilt and destroyed again and again, in what became known as the Muskrat and Beaver Wars. The clashes continued, with some violence, for more than thirty years.

The conflict ended in 1871 when a court ruled that no more dams could be constructed. Downstream, with the flow diverted, the mill operations closed and industry in the town of Hampton died. The water turned fetid and more than 100 people got malaria from an infestation of mosquitoes. The Beavers had truly lost the war.

It had became increasingly clear to upstream farm owners that for the muck lands to survive as arable acreage and not revert to a bog, it was (and still is) critical that serious and supervised drainage occur across the entire territory. Drainage ditches had been dug by landowners since the 1770s, but by the early 1900s it was obvious that community organized drainage was essential. Several attempts were made but it wasn't until 1933 that a formal petition for the formation of a drainage improvement district was filed with the state Water Power and Control Commission (WPCC) who undertook to do a survey of 18,000 acres of muck lands. They drew up a detailed, comprehensive plan for 51 named and numbered ditches to remove water from the entire valley and drain it into the Wallkill River or its creeks.

Part of the rush to have a drainage district formed with a properly mapped survey was a result of the election in 1933 of President Franklin D. Roosevelt. On assuming office he promptly created an army of jobless men to work on emergency conservation measures – a remedy for the dire unemployment that followed the Great Depression.

At Roosevelt's behest a bill creating a Civilian Conservation Corps (CCC) quickly passed and the search for "shovel ready" work projects began. The Army Corps of Engineers, an agency under the Department of Defense charged with major engineering, design, and construction management – usually associated with waterways – submitted a plan to improve the Wallkill River for drainage and flood control. To be eligible for the federal jobs project a local authority had to be involved. As fast as they possibly could the towns of Goshen, Minisink, Warwick and Waywayanda got together to create the Wallkill Valley Drainage Improvement District (WVDID), authorized by the New York State Department of Conservation Water Power and Control Commission.

The Wallkill River improvement project was accepted by the Public Works Administration and in May, 1935, more than 1,000 men moved into four CCC camps scattered around the muck lands of Orange County. Among their objectives was to improve the existing Cheechunk Canal, construct another 5.5 mile channel cutting off 8.5 miles of zig-zags in the river's course, and install rip-rapping – overlapping layers of stones in the bed and banks. The work was designed to increase the water flow from 800 cubic feet per second to 8,000 cubic feet per second.

Meantime, in 1935, the Wallkill Valley Drainage Improvement District became legal, with the powers of a public corporation, able to acquire or sell property, to sue or be sued, to make contracts, exercise eminent domain, make assessments and issue taxation, and do all necessary to accomplish its obligations. A month later the WPCC made an agreement with the Federal Government on behalf of the drainage district for work to start on the 51 "Commissioners' Ditches." These are the critical arteries that run throughout the entire valley to this day, and without which the Black Dirt would revert to the Drowned Lands and agricultural productivity would promptly die.

Meantime, the CCC project ran out of money after a year, well before work was completed. The drainage district, with other representatives from the region, went to Washington DC to appear before the flood control committee at the Senate Commerce Committee and appealed for more funds. They were successful, so work continued until 1937 when the CCC – which numbered 2,000 men by then - finished the project, closed their camps and moved away.

Tom Pahucki, who for 21 years until 2013 was an Orange County Legislative Representative, and took the river on as a personal crusade, argues that the work was purely for unemployment relief – that was the only interest in the region. And that's why the upstream portion of the Wallkill River still writhes a jagged course through the muck lands, getting more sluggish every year.

The first recorded catastrophic flood was in 1955, when hurricanes Connie and Diane coincided, submerging the valley at depths unprecedented in human memory at the time. Locals remember it as "biblical" in scale. They would recall with awe how the uplands of the valley reverted to islands in a vast lake and like the early Native Americans, residents paddled about in boats.

After a few more serious floods the Congressman for the region at the time, Ben Gilman (R), got together with farmers including Charlie Lain, the sod farmer whose land was bordered by the river, and Ted Sobiech, Sr., Lain's neighbor, and asked the Federal Government to get involved again. They persuaded the government to accept that it had authority over a river that ran through two states (New York and New Jersey) and three counties, (Sussex, Orange and Ulster) and therefore, it had to take responsibility for the overflow.

In 1983 the Army Corps of Engineers studied the situation and then recommended "channel improvement" in the twisted upstream section of the river that runs through the Black Dirt at a then cost of $15 million. Many farmers interpreted "channel improvement" to mean dredging, which usually implies deepening and/or removing sediment. Many in the Black Dirt valley, including farmers, still believe that "dredging" is the solution to the flooding problem. But others argue that dredging is done to improve navigation, not drainage or flood control.

Cost constraints placed on the Corps led them to take the cheaper option of clearing away dead trees and debris to speed up water flowing through the valley – a job that was completed in 1985. The Corps knew it would not fix the flooding forever, partly because of the continuing land surface subsidence that results from the continual oxidation in the organic black soil. They predicted that it would eliminate a 10-year flood (a flood of the severity that only occurs every ten years.)

In 2005, twenty years after the Army Corps packed up and left, the river started flooding. It then flooded seven times in the next seven years (twice in 2005, in 2007 and 2010, and three times in 2011). All the while farmers pleaded for help.

After April 2007 when a nor'easter drenched the region, and the Wallkill poured into the farmlands, the Army Corps did look at both the Wallkill River and Rondout Creek in Ulster County, closer to the Hudson River. They recommended a detailed study to look at appropriate improvements. The study, they said, would take about four years and cost an estimated $2.5 million.

Frustrated Black Dirt farmers note the irony that Orange County is home to West Point Military Academy, the nation's finest army officer training facility, where graduates include army engineers. "When the army is attacked by an enemy, they immediately launch a counter attack. But when the farmers are attacked by an enemy, the Army Engineers want to do a four year study!" comments one frustrated farmer, who lost hundreds of acres of crops when Hurricane Irene caused the Wallkill to flood in 2011.

It's hard to find anyone in the farming community who believes there is reason or time for a four-year study, and especially after the catastrophic flooding of 2011. After that event, County Legislator Pahucki was determined to get a portion of the river cleared of trees that were considered to be blocking the flow. However, the New York State Department of Environmental Conservation (DEC) claimed the trees he wanted to remove were areas where bugs might lurk – bugs that were forage for the Indiana Bat, which has been listed under the Endangered Species Act since 1967.

These tiny bats weigh about a quarter of an ounce, yet have a wingspan of nine to eleven inches, according to the U.S. Fish and Wildlife Service website list of Endangered Species. They became endangered because humans were disturbing their winter hibernation habitat, a number of caves elsewhere in the state. White Nose Syndrome, a disease that has killed bats across the U.S., was also killing off the tiny, local bats. In summer they roost under the peeling bark of dead and dying trees and feed on a variety of flying insects found along rivers or lakes and in uplands.

Pahucki argues that the trees are "potential," not real forage, and thus do not qualify for protection under the Endangered Species Act. "They care more about lizards and turtles and frogs than farmers," said Pahucki. He points out that it is the fond wish of some environmentalists that the Wallkill valley revert to swampland for birds and wildlife. They are antagonistic towards Black Dirt conventional farmers – seeing them as environmental polluters – and consider flooding to be an ecological benefit, even though a flood plain would remove a food plain

Pahucki's team, believing they had permission from the DEC to remove trees impeding the flow in an upstream portion of the riverbed, got an Orange County Executive Order which allocated $35,500 to go ahead with tree-clearing before the 2012 spring rains. An excavation team swiftly – extremely swiftly, to avoid any confrontation with environmentalists – cut down and removed about 500 swamp maples that had taken root in the river.

This furtive move was applauded by some Black Dirt farmers, who see Pahucki as a hero. But it enraged the property owners, environmentalists and some neighboring town and county officials who claim that public funds were used for an action that was unnecessary and possibly illegal.

There is another, serious issue complicating the river problem: In 1974 Orange County (with State approval) built a 75-acre landfill that is bordered by the Wallkill River near Denton. In his research study titled *The Wallkill River, The Cheechunk Canal and the Orange County Landfill*, former TV journalism professor Fred Isseks, Ph.D, claims that Mafia-controlled garbage carting companies dumped in the landfill toxic waste from the New York metro area, including New Jersey. Landfill workers, police and even politicians averted their eyes, says Isseks. Choc-a-bloc with seven million tons of garbage, including illegal toxins, the landfill was closed in 1992.

There is now visible evidence that the Orange County Landfill is gradually bulging into the river. Concerns have been raised by the Army Corps of Engineers and others that efforts to dredge or widen the river to increase the flow and lessen flooding might risk polluting water for communities downstream.

The water quality is supposed to be constantly monitored by the county for toxic leaks. The county initially claimed there was no evidence of seepage from the landfill, though Isseks's research project showed video of orange colored fluid at the surface of the river bank. But in a major blow, in May 2015 the county admitted that elevated ammonia levels had been found in groundwater seepage on the banks of the Wallkill in the Cheechunk Canal area. In response to state DEC concerns about contamination of the Wallkill, the county agreed to pump groundwater from beneath the landfill to address the problem, setting aside $1.4 million to deal with it.

Late summer of 2015 environmentalist Sue Cleaver broadcast online pictures she said she'd taken of more orange colored leachate at about five spots on the banks of the Wallkill River at the Cheechunk Canal. All the grim news received very little local media attention. The measure undertaken by the County is unlikely to satisfy environmentalists and the news will certainly complicate plans to increase the flow of the river.

Still, most people in the region concur that something more has to be done so the river accepts normal seasonal springtime rains without flooding. "Though, with global warming, 'normal' doesn't exist," says Chip Lain, the farmer who bought and then expanded his father Charlie Lain's sod farm that flanks the Wallkill River. Chip says that in the past it took six inches of rain for the river to overflow into his fields. "Now it just takes four."

There is no consensus in the farming community and among local river cognoscenti, who have studied its flow for decades, on exactly what that something is. A key person in the river debate is Kevin Sumner, manager of the Orange County Soil and Water Conservation District, the body which is overseeing a $2 million State grant to implement flood mitigation measures. An engineering firm was hired to investigate, research and report back to a committee that includes at least six farmers who own muck land alongside the river.

Sumner, who has a degree in Biological Science and is a Certified Professional in Erosion and Sediment Control (CPESC) and Stormwater Quality (CPSWQ), has spent 30 years studying the Wallkill River and Black Dirt soils. He takes a different approach:

> The solution isn't fixing the river because the river isn't broken
> – it's doing what rivers do on the bed of a glacial lake. The
> approach should lean towards modifying the river because it
> flows through a flood plain where agriculture occurs. I think
> most growers realize nothing will prevent flooding after extreme
> weather events. We must focus on the moderate, 10-year frequency
> event – 5.5 inches in 24 hours. That's what we'd like to control,
> and the jury is still out on our ability to do that.

One little-known aspect of the problem is that the fall, or slope, is only about one foot per mile over the 10-mile run through the muck lands. With so shallow an incline, floodwater is not going to stay in a channel, explains Sumner.

At the Middletown, NY, office of the OC Soil and Water Conservation District, shelves and desks are scattered with rocks and a varied assemblage of potted plants. The function of his department is rooted in concern for the environment and some farmers consider Sumner biased against farming. Should the Black Dirt valley revert to drowned lands? "I would never recommend it," he said. "In a world of trade-offs, we can grow high quality vegetables here, and as long as people are willing to farm, we must do what we can to support them."

Sumner is a man buffeted from all sides by the passionately held but divergent views of affected farmers on how to remedy the flooding problem. He says that after initial reports by the engineers, the committee has decided to pursue two flood-control measures: One is to dig deep grooves in two rock ledges that jut into the river, slowing the flow. This remedy would improve flow but the effects would dissipate quickly so the majority of farmers downstream would not see much benefit.

The second option, now favored by most of the farmers on the committee, is to leave the river in its present course but to create wide "benches" on either side of the bank. "This approach lets the river function as a river. If the banks are 10-12 feet high now, we go six feet up the bank and then cut a bench 90 feet wide at that level, on either side, for the full length of the river in the flood plain. Modern engineering models created by the Army Corps and accepted throughout the industry as a means of measuring flow tell us that benches have the most benefit."

These 90-foot "benches" on either side of the river could become spots for riparian enjoyment, fishing, picnics and walks – except when the river floods! Or they might revert to swamp, perhaps filled with birdlife. For the full eight miles, cost estimates range from a $1.3m a mile to $10m a mile– in either case, far more money than remains from the State grant.

Another popular option is to extend the Cheechunk Canal through the meandering upstream segment of the river that was never dealt with during the improvements undertaken in the 1930s. Sumner says: "The 1930s technology (the canal) lowers the water level by 10 inches, while the bench system gives us 20 inches."

No federal funds have yet been made available for flood prevention in the Black Dirt basin. But Congressman Sean Patrick Maloney (D-18th) had language put in the 2014 Farm Bill that recognized the importance of the Black Dirt region – wording which might allow for special funding for flood prevention.

However, Sumner's department has been moving ahead, applying for permits and grant money so work can begin as soon as possible. The fact that the money would be used to benefit agriculture, not bridges and highways, or the environment, might disqualify the project from eligibility for a number of the target funds – a consideration that clearly frustrates Sumner, hurts the Black Dirt region's flood control prospects, and thus threatens production of millions of mouthfuls of healthy fresh vegetables.

Black Dirt farmer Joe Morgiewicz, whose 160-acre family farm near the Cheechunk Canal is low-lying and extremely vulnerable to flooding, is among the farmers who attribute some of the new river overflow to development in the region during the 1980s and 1990s which removed pasture without planning for where the new runoff would go. Like his brothers Dave and Dan, partners in Morgiewicz Farms, he is a volunteer fireman in the district and points out that when the new fire house was built in 2009, septic fields were built beneath the property so that rainwater would leach into the ground and not form runoff which would increase water levels in the river.

Michael Sweeton, current Warwick Town Supervisor whose constituency includes the Black Dirt plain, agrees that some of the new flooding might result from the extensive property development that took place in neighboring areas of New Jersey in the 1980s and 1990s, bringing blacktop, paving and rooftops. These new impervious surfaces inevitably increase the volume and the speed of water entering the Wallkill and its creeks.

Sweeton says there has to be a sensible balance between the "we can't do anything" attitude of some oversight authorities in the past, and farmers who would dredge the river with unknown consequences for those downstream. "Farming here is an important industry for millions of people and something must be done," he warns.

Although they tend to be independent-minded, and fiscally conservative, Black Dirt farmers consider the cost of preventing the catastrophic flooding of an important supply region for fresh, healthy food for the millions of people in the area an appropriate use of tax-payer money.

In his 2014 research study named above, Prof. Fred Isseks notes: "No one seems to be paying attention except the farmers." In fact, they feel abandoned, he says.

"They believe they have an understanding with the government to maintain the canal because the job is too big for the farmers to undertake themselves. If you want farms, they argue, you have to help us protect them. The farmers want the government to dredge the canal, clear the banks, and open and maintain the feeder channels. They are waiting for any kind of help, even though it's generally understood that nothing short of a massive engineering project will solve the problem."

"The Terrorist Among Us"

Past flooding damage and the unchecked, continuing threat from the river have, over the years, persuaded many families to abandon farming. Among them are Tom and Robin Sobiech, who live on top of Merritts Island in an elegant, landmark house that was built in the 1700s and once was owned by the "Onion King" Vince Kosuga. The property looks over the Mission Land tract where three generations of the Sobiech family grew onions.

Tom Sobiech recalls: "My Dad, Ted, who was born in 1933, had about 900 acres, growing onions, lettuce and celery, and 90 acres of alfalfa. In 1973, when I was 14 or 15, I went with my dad and a delegation of farmers to DC to see our congressman, Ben Gilman (R). We went to ask for money to do something about the flooding of the Wallkill River."

They did not get the help they hoped for. "The river, up to the 1980s, was not too bad. Then it began to get worse every year. In the late 1980s and early 90s other states began to ship onions here. So now we had not just weather and flooding but new competition and a lot of farms went out of business. People blame it on various factors, but it was mainly the river, the flooding." In 1986 Ted Sobiech filed for bankruptcy.

"When the floods came they displaced everything," said Tom. "You find fish dead in the ditches and the wildlife drowned. The Government does nothing even though this is the biggest produce growing region near the largest city in America. It's the government's river. It's government negligence for not fixing it. You can't farm next to a river you can't predict. It's like living next to a terrorist. You never know when it's coming for you."

Tom Sobiech says that after being wiped out by floods in 10 out of 12 years he and his wife decided in 2010 to get out of farming altogether. Growing 100 acres of onions at the time he sold his farmland and went into the gas pipeline industry where two of his three sons have joined him, working mainly with environmental protection issues. He says they love the work. "You see, when my kids were young I told them not to get into farming, and

I'm glad none of them did."

The possibility that the Federal Government would indeed be playing a major role in the lives of the Black Dirt farmers – in an unwelcome way – arose in 2014 when the Environmental Protection Agency (EPA) proposed to extend their oversight authority under the Clean Water Act to include ditches, drains and ponds, wetlands and floodplains across the U.S.. The outrage from farmers around the entire U.S. was instant and effective, forcing the EPA to withdraw some provisions, and assure farmers that the proposed bill would not bring all ditches on farms under federal jurisdiction. Skeptical, the U.S. Farm Bureau asked Congress to intervene.

In the Black Dirt, farmers already beleaguered by paperwork and permits involved in maintenance of miles of drainage ditches as well as the spectrum of regulations governing chemical use, were deeply concerned by the possible expansion of federal reach. Chip Lain, whose farm is drained by more than 50 miles of ditches, said he was no longer concerned that the original proposal would go ahead. "But if it does, if they do what we fear most, it would shut the farming community down."

Onion farmer Chris Pawelski's concern was that any new regulations under the EPA's expanded reach would be administered by bureaucrats who knew nothing about farming, let alone the details and technicalities involved in digging, dredging and maintaining ditches. "Sometimes you have just one hour's notice before you have to make a move on the farm. How are you going to get a permit from a bureaucracy in one hour? Ludicrous!"

Wildlife Refuge vs Farmers

The sense that federal authorities might be indifferent – if not adversarial – to Black Dirt farmers was confirmed for many of them in 2008 after the Wallkill River National Wildlife Refuge in New Jersey violated its original mandate and expanded into Black Dirt farm lands.

Congress established this beautiful refuge in 1990 to "preserve and enhance lands and waters in a manner that conserves the natural diversity of fish, wildlife, plants and their habitats for present and future generations." Most of the 5,100-acre wildlife haven is in Sussex, New Jersey, spreading on either side of nine miles of the Wallkill River. The expansion of the refuge over the state line into New York was seen as a farmland-grab, incorporating 450 acres of Black Dirt that was actively growing onions, corn, soybeans and squash.

Expansion started when the Liberty Sod farm, adjacent to the Wildlife Refuge, came up for sale. Half the farm was in New Jersey, half in New York's muck lands. The terms of sale were that the buyer – the refuge - had to purchase the whole property, because the New York portion was too small to be viable as a sod farm. Thus occurred the first incursion into the Black Dirt.

The U.S. Fish and Wildlife Authority, which runs the refuge, then drew up plans to further extend into the Black Dirt, a move supported by some local Warwick area environmentalists. But at a meeting in the Warwick Town Hall Black Dirt farmers overwhelmingly opposed the Wildlife Refuge expansions. The Pine Island Chamber of Commerce sent a protest letter to local members of congress, summing up the farming community objections.

"Starting in 1773, and repeatedly over almost 235 years, public funds and efforts have gone towards draining "The Drowned Lands", in order to make the rich soil suitable for agriculture. Reverting farmland to wetlands is in complete contradiction of the course of local history and the goal of keeping farmland productive. It would create weed-infested swamps in land farmers are struggling to drain."

The objections were ignored and the expansion went ahead.

When a neighboring Black Dirt property owned by the Unification Church (the "Moonies") came up for sale, the Tennessee Pipeline Company bought it and then deeded it to the Wildlife Refuge in exchange for a pipeline right of way in the New Jersey portion of the refuge. The move is considered by the farmers to have been a deal by the refuge to get control of more of the Black Dirt farmland in New York State without arousing farmer's objections.

On a crisp fall day in the wildlife refuge beside a picturesque nature trail called the Liberty Loop, U.S. Fish and Wildlife manger, Mike Horne. talked about the situation. He looked out over Liberty Marsh, once the 150-acre plot that was the Liberty Sod Farm. It had almost completely reverted to grassy wetlands, with a few boggy patches of black soil still visible.

Horne said the big issue for him at the WRWR was "water management," a euphemism for flooding. The Wallkill River, running through the refuge, floods twice a year, overflowing the dikes built to retain it. "A part of the challenge in the past has been a war with our neighbors, the farmers," said Horne. "But now the relationship is very cooperative."

His closest neighbor is local historian and farmer John Ruszkiewicz, who opposes the presence of the refuge in the muck lands, but has done ditch cleaning on refuge land to solve drainage problems on his own land. Horne said the refuge management doesn't have the equipment or expertise to drain the ditches.

"It's a balancing act. We manipulate the water for the benefit of the wildlife – that's why we are here, " said Horne. He suggests, however, that there might be ways the refuge could lessen the impact of floodwaters on nearby farms. "My goal is to cobble together something that works for all of us."

However, farmers argue that the refuge had no reason to expand into Orange County at all because wildlife and bird species are already in abundance in the region – and particularly the section of the Wildlife Refuge south of the New York State line. Leonard DeBuck, the farmer dedicated to sustainability and environmentally sound farming practices, says flocks of geese from the wildlife refuge nearby feed in the wetlands then fly over his fields, defecating seeds for strange plant species that severely test his pesticide-free principles.

Some nearby farmers complain that deer, which flourish in the refuge, create health hazards by wandering into neighboring farms. Deer feces have, on multiple occasions, been determined as the source of E. coli contamination of produce.

So its no wonder that many in the Black Dirt farming community feel their government and its agencies place little value on their role as produce providers for the tristate region. Until the public becomes informed, and therefore alarmed, there will be little motivation to provide the funds to make the Black Dirt valley flood free and dependably agriculturally viable.

Flooding, however, is not the only serious threat facing the farmers of the Black Dirt region. The dire shortage of farm workers, exacerbated by inadequate immigrant work visa regulations, is already a serious threat to farming throughout the United States – and particularly in this agricultural area where both the crops and requirement to get them to market fresh every day are highly labor intensive. ■

CHAPTER SEVEN: FARM HANDS

"...the best way to protect farm workers is to work with farmers, not vilify them."

Second to the possibility of being annihilated by a catastrophic flood, nothing threatens the Black Dirt farms more than the shortage of labor to work in the fields and help bring produce to market. In the 2013 season only 60% of the labor requirements were met, costing millions in possible profits in the muck lands and potential food for markets. On many farms produce had to be left to rot in the fields. Again in 2014 and 2015 farmers were unable to get the number of workers they needed. The shortage has become so widespread and acute in the northeast that before harvest time apple farmers from upstate New York have sent recruiters into the Black Dirt to furtively hire workers off the produce farms, promising better pay.

In recent years and continuing into 2015, the shortage of workers from Latin America heading to agricultural jobs in the U.S. was exacerbated by the dangers posed at the Mexican border by the growing power of the drug mafia – a condition of lawless brutality. Those trying to enter the U.S. might face Los Zetas, a widespread, savage Mexican cartel who now make a high percentage of their annual billions by forcing migrants to carry drugs across the border or kidnapping for ransom migrants bound for the U.S. to work (and killing them if ransom demands aren't met.) "Coyotes" promising safe passage and or escort into the U.S. for fees as high as $7,000 have themselves become so corrupt they are high risk. The corruption has spread across the border into the U.S. where, it is reported, some border officials are collaborators, and cartels have infiltrated gangs in the U.S..

In short, stricter security at the border has made migrants more vulnerable to cartels. As a result far fewer migrants are prepared to risk the journey. So called "border security" to prevent migrants entering the U.S. illegally is now actually being aided by the criminal Los Zetas and other gangsters. What can Americans do? Stop the drug use that creates the demand, or legalize drugs so the black market that gives existence to the cartels disappears.

Added to the discouragement from coming to the U.S. to work on farms posed by stricter U.S. border controls, and the security threats posed by criminals in Mexico, is the fact that more jobs are now available in that country, in part because U.S. agricultural and other industries have moved their operations across the border to take advantage of cheaper labor there.

The Partnership for a New American Economy, a non-partisan group that supports a looser immigration policy, reports that in the U.S. the decline in the number of farm workers has reduced fruit and vegetable production by 9.5%, the equivalent of $3.1 billion a year. (Wall Street Journal, August 12, 2015)

Maire Ullrich of the CCE says that labor could well become the #1 problem for farmers. "We need 30% more hands, now. We have tried patching the failed immigration law with the use of Vocational-Technical School students, refugees, the unemployed…" She shook her head.

Alex Kocot, whose 400 acre Harvest Queen farm includes 170 acres of onions and more than 90 acres of labor intensive baby greens, believes that a shortage of farm workers is indeed the biggest threat to farmers in the region. He has a dedicated team of 16 Mexicans – "one of the best crews around, they are like my sons" – who have worked for him under legal work visas for many years. But the documentation process is so arduous for them and the journey from their homes in Mexico so risky he ponders what will happen when they no longer want to make the 3,500 mile journey to his farm. "Take away immigrant labor, the food supply will fall apart. No Americans want to do the work."

It's a U.S.-wide problem. Americans don't want to work in farm fields, whether in the Black Dirt, the South, the West or the Northern states. Migrants are the vast majority of farm workers in the United States (and in many other countries). But the main cause of the farm labor shortage is the complicated, inefficient, inadequate immigration law that bedevils agriculture across the United States, and especially on the labor-intensive, seasonal produce farms like those that dominate in the Black Dirt valley.

A well crafted Immigration Bill that would enable farm workers to enter the U.S. legally, work on farms and then return home, has been stalled by the political stalemate in Washington DC since early 2014. In 2015 the immigration bill was again blocked by party politics, while millions of workers and farmers with their livelihoods at stake, were rendered frustrated spectators. Congressman Sean Patrick Maloney (D), who represents the Black Dirt region, is urging all Americans to keep pressure on their representatives so that a bill that includes a practical, efficient visa for agricultural workers can become law.

The Department of Agriculture counts at least one million farm workers in the United States. According to the Migrant Farm Worker Justice Project 85% of farm workers are immigrants, and up to 70% of them are undocumented. And that makes them vulnerable to abuse. Notorious abuses have been exposed in Florida, Georgia and other parts of the United States in recent years. Those incidents included unpaid work, physical assault, forced prostitution, illegal child labor and dangerous working conditions.

There were abuses in the northeast in the 1960s, as documented in the famed and shocking Edwin R. Morrow TV documentary, *Harvest of Shame*, which led to the enactment by New York State of an array of legal protections for farm workers. Those laws are in force today, continuing to help protect farm workers, documented or not.

However, in more than 30 years there have been no allegations of systematic farm worker abuse in the Black Dirt region. Stash Grajewski, Director of the Farm Workers Community Centre, that serves the interests of farm workers in the valley, says that he knows of no confirmed cases of institutional abuse of workers in the muck lands in his 35-year tenure. He knew of an instance when a farmer of Chinese heritage had failed to follow regulations on paying his field workers and several farmers mentioned a Mexican farmer who was reported to authorities because the living conditions for his workers were not consistent with the regulations. As for "horrendous" and "abhorrent" conditions, it was hard to find anyone with examples.

Two Sisters of the Divine Compassion, Catholic nuns who have, for 25 years, run the Mustard Seed Migrant Ministry in the Black Dirt region, providing care for farm workers and their children, talk with warmth of the farmers of the valley. They report that farmers have given money year after year to help keep the ministry going. Their operation, which serves at least 65 migrant children aged from five to late teens, is dependent on community funding.

Sister Pam Wagner, who is the co-director with Sister Fran Liston, said "our experience is that the farmers here are good people who care about their farm workers. They are hands on and often work beside their workers. You might get a few farmers who are not kind to their workers," she said, "but you also get farm hands who are not up to par... it's the human condition."

However, there are activists and elected officials – mostly in urban areas – who frequently and publicly describe the conditions of all farm workers in all of New York State as "horrendous" and "abhorrent," claims loudly reported even though they are unsupported by evidence. Harking back 55 years to the *Harvest of Shame* documentary and more recent abuses in southern states, these claims arouse profound prejudices against farmers and create the impression that all migrant farm workers are underpaid and exploited in ways that would shock the public if they knew the details, but no details are provided.

Orange County farmers report that they are frequently subjected to insinuations that they mistreat those who work on their farms. Paul Ruszkiewicz, president of the Orange County Vegetable Growers Association, says the term "slave owner" is bandied about indiscriminately as a description of farmers' relationship with their workers, especially in activist literature.

No one disputes that work in the Black Dirt fields is grueling and the pay is often low compared with many other job categories. However, staff at the Farm Workers Community Center report that farm workers in this region are paid an average $10 an hour, above the minimum wage which is now $8.75. Some make $20 an hour for skilled harvesting.

But whatever the pay, in the muck lands, as elsewhere in the United States, very few Americans want to do the work. You understand why if you read *Farm*

Hands: Hard Work and Hard Lessons from Western New York Fields, in which journalist Tom Rivers describes how he became a farm laborer, working alongside Mexicans and Haitians (who believed Americans wouldn't do farm
work because they were too lazy.) He writes that his experience working on
a variety of farms taught him that there are no stereo-typical good guys and
bad guys in farming – just farmers and farm workers, interdependent,
equally trying hard to make a living.

Grajewski at the Farm Workers' Community Center tells how 30 years
ago when he was so fit he could run 3.2 miles in 17 minutes, he pondered
the question of why Americans didn't want to work in the fields. The farmer
he was visiting invited him to try himself. "I started weeding at 7.30 am and
by 11 am I'd almost collapsed. It was even mentally grueling – you must just
concentrate on weeds. If you think of anything else you can't do the job."

He points out that the tradition of immigrants doing the toughest jobs
is a worldwide phenomenon. "Local populations won't do farm work. I remember seeing Haitians working in the field in the neighboring Dominican
Republic because the locals wouldn't. In Germany the farm work has traditionally been done by Turks. In Italy it's Africans. France used poor
Spaniards and Spain's farms are worked by Moroccans."

In Costa Rica, 80% of the farm workers on the coffee plantations are
from neighboring Nicaragua.

Take Our Jobs!

Many of those strongly opposed to any legal work permits for migrant
farm workers claim that they are taking jobs from Americans at a time of
high unemployment. Cut welfare, some argue, and Americans removed
from "government hand-outs" will be motivated to work on the farms. Suggestions for immigration law reforms include a stipulation that all jobs must
first be offered to Americans before they can be taken by migrant workers.

The United Farm Workers (UFW) devised a plan to disprove that migrants are taking jobs in agriculture away from willing Americans. They
launched a "Take Our Jobs" campaign, inviting Americans to apply for the
80,000 farm jobs available. They advised:

> *Job may include using hand tools such as knives, hoes,*
> *shovels, etc. Duties may include tilling the soil, transplanting,*
> *weeding, thinning, picking, cutting, sorting & packing of*

harvested produce. May set up & operate irrigation equip.
Work is performed outside in all weather conditions
(Summertime 90+ degree weather) & is physically
demanding requiring workers to bend, stoop, lift & carry
up to 50 lbs on a regular basis.

After three months three million people had visited the website, www.takeourjobs.com, but just 8,600 were interested in farm jobs. Many of them asked for perks that are associated with regular fulltime jobs, such as health and pension benefits. In the end, only seven Americans who applied during the campaign were doing farm jobs.

Enforcement of laws against illegal employment of undocumented workers have had serious consequences. In Georgia, the HB 87 immigration enforcement law, passed in 2011, gave police the power to demand documentation from suspects when they were detained for other possible infringements, and it penalized businesses which hired illegal workers. As a result, farm workers avoided the state and crops rotted in the fields. The labor shortages cost an estimated $140 million in farm losses.

Immigration Policy

The Immigration Reform and Control Act of 1986 (IRCA) prohibits employers from hiring and employing workers for employment in the United States knowing that these workers are not authorized to work in the U.S.. For every employee, employers must complete a Form I-9 which contains detailed identification and employment authorization information. There are harsh fines for employers who do not get the I-9 Form completed, or who knowingly accept false documents. However, getting the I-9 information verified by the appropriate government body is so slow that seasonal farm workers have frequently moved on before the documentation is ascertained to be false or valid.

Tens of thousands of workers acquire false documents so they can work on U.S. farms pretending to be legal. Many tens of thousands more do not come to the U.S. to work in agriculture because the process of getting a legal work visa is so arduous and, as pointed out earlier, the venture into the U.S. is so dangerous. Agriculture Secretary Tom Vilsak has said the only hope to stave off an economic disaster for the American agricultural sector is an overhaul of immigration policy.

Unlike other countries such as Canada, which has a strict but functioning guest worker program serving the agricultural sector, the existing U.S. system is complicated and extremely burdensome for employers. The current temporary agricultural workers' visa, the H-2A, designed to allow seasonal workers to come into the U.S. to work on U.S. farms, is efficient only for a few short-window harvests like apples, but for the majority it is considered excessively burdensome and expensive.

There is not enough infrastructure to process the applications for the roughly one million seasonal workers who would be applying for the visas. Applications can take more than three months to be fulfilled – which means farmers might have no workers at planting time, while would-be workers remain in their home countries, without work, waiting for legal visas.

Produce farmer Frank Dagele said he was this year (2015) applying for H-2A visas for foreign workers for the first time because he couldn't get enough workers in the U.S. - and no Americans want to do the job. "It's so complicated," he said of the H-2A visa process, "you have to use a lawyer."

The process is also burdensome – and dangerous – even for workers with legal work visas, as farm owner Alex Kocot reports. He acquires the H-2A visa for his crew of 16 Mexicans. They must travel thousands of miles, which can take a week, just to get their documentation. Recently they hired a bus to make transport back to their job in the U.S. safer and simpler. Just five miles short of the U.S. border they were stopped by armed men who searched them. Kocot said the work team was only allowed to proceed after they had each paid the armed men $15.

A national survey conducted by the National Council of Agricultural Employers of H-2A employers under the current rules showed that administrative delays result in workers arriving on average 22 days after the date of need, causing an economic loss of nearly $320 million for farms that hire H-2A workers.

Farmers using the H-2A visa are required to pay for their agricultural workers' transport to the U.S. from their home country, their housing and other benefits. There are steep fines for growers who violate the many rules under the H-2A program. The truth is that an estimated 80% of farmers don't use it – in the Black Dirt and nationwide.

Black Dirt farmer Lenny DeBuck, who has employed the same six Mexicans, almost all from the same family, for more than 15 years, is one of a minority of farmers in the region who still use the H-2A visa, despite the complications and frustrations. He does it for the benefit and safety of his workers – so they can cross the border legally, and avoid using the coyotes who demand exorbitant fees to get them into the U.S. and arrange work contracts.

"My workers are like friends who rely on me for employment so they can support their families – no different than the way I depend on them for the work they do that helps me support my family. It's a co-dependency of trust," he says. "Laborers want consistency – they shouldn't be treated like a commodity, or like shady individuals. They are just people who want to work."

What makes matters worse, says Paul Ruszkiewicz of the Vegetable Growers Association (VGA), is that since the enforcement crackdown on the border with Mexico in recent years, and the problems getting into the U.S. legally, many of the undocumented migrant farm workers are fearful that if they return home after the harvest, they won't be able to get back into the U.S.. As a result, they stay in the U.S. illegally. "Granting amnesty isn't the issue here. Most of them want to go home, and would if they could return to the U.S. properly entitled to work," he said.

An alternative being proposed (early 2015) by house Republicans is E-Verify, which forces employers to instantly verify the legality of their prospective workers' documentation, with penalties for violations. Farmers adamantly oppose E-Verify since the overwhelming majority of farm workers in the United States are undocumented and the existing guest worker system is grossly inadequate. Under E-Verify farmers would face crippling labor shortages or risk fines for knowingly employing undocumented workers.

The Ag Workforce Coalition, which includes Western Growers, the U.S. Apple Association, the National Council of Agricultural Employers, the Florida Fruit & Vegetable Association, the United Fresh Produce Association and other agriculture groups, wrote a letter to House leaders asking for provisions for agriculture.

"The path forward is clear — Congress should pass a solution for agriculture that addresses both our current agricultural workforce and creates a new guest worker program to meet future needs and only then implement a mandatory E-Verify program," the group said in a statement.

Regulations

Undocumented workers in every country and category of work are vulnerable to abuse. The fear that dominates their everyday lives gives employers extra power in all the industries that are highly dependent on migrant workers, including manufacturing, construction and the hospitality industry – not just agriculture. The fact is that in all industries a few employers abuse that power, so relying on employer integrity and decency obviously isn't sufficient.

Motivated partly by that vulnerability, and the history of farm worker mistreatment in the past, federal and state laws – and especially in New York State – have created a cocoon of protections for all agricultural workers. Few people outside farming are aware of the extensive network of rules set up to benefit and protect farm workers in New York. From wage contracts to working conditions, health and safety standards and housing facilities, the farmers must conform to a morass of regulations.

Paul Ruszkiewicz of the VGA says that farm owners don't complain about compliance with the regulations. Sensitive to the negative assumptions already made about farmers' treatment of their field workers they realize that any abuse by one farmer would be a slur on the reputation of all the muck land farmers. Growers have called the Department of Labor or Department of Health to report suspected violations by another farmer.

To ensure compliance, the New York State Department of Labor sends inspectors to do checks of accounting records, labor contracts, working and housing conditions, and more. Self- appointed monitors from not-for-profit activist groups also sporadically arrive in the Black Dirt to check on the conditions and treatment of farm workers. In the 1980s and 90s these often unannounced inspections came to be widely viewed as a form of harassment, based on prejudices against farm owners.

Unscheduled inspections of farms in the Black Dirt continue to this day, and not always with courtesy. "I have no problem with inspectors," says Frank Dagele of Dagele Brothers Farm. "But they don't have to behave like the Gestapo. People from the Department of Labor arrive un-announced, are arrogant and treat us like criminals. Would they do that if they were inspecting work conditions at the local utility company?" Dagele's description of his experience with the inspectors was echoed by other farmers.

He said the inspectors always demand to see his books but have never found anything wrong with his accounting records. "Why are we being treated like this? Is it because we are farmers? This is federally funded harassment."

Frank Dagele is one of three brothers running the 550-acre farm that was started as a small subsistence operation by his great grandparents about 100 years ago. At the farm on a fall Saturday farm forklifts were buzzing and the sense of harvest urgency was present in the chilly air. Sitting in his farm office, Dagele said he was just as angry with those who don't appreciate the work that migrants do in the United States as he is with those who harass him because he employs them. "Contrary to all the pundits, no American wants to work on farms."

While travelling out of state he saw an American politician's campaign advertisement which suggested that migrant workers were maggots, coming to feed on the U.S.. He was outraged. "These are people who grow our crops, prepare our food in restaurants, mow our lawns and wash our cars."

There has never been a complaint against Dagele Brothers Farm by farm workers and people in the Black Dirt region described Frank Dagele as a pillar of the community. Even when it was not required by any law, Dagele provided free accommodation for his farm workers. This meant he had to follow the regulations controlling occupancy rates, showers, TV's, and kitchen facilities.

The rules and the spot inspections and fines consequent to providing housing have led about half of all farmers in the region to close down and sometimes demolish the accommodation they once provided free for farm workers. Farm owners' stories include vandalism by farm workers, fines for infringing regulations, and exasperation with the frequent, sometimes furtive, "harassment" by official and unofficial inspectors.

Now, workers on the 50% of farms that do not provide accommodation must find un-regulated housing elsewhere, where they must pay rent, and hope they can find transport to and from work – a significant problem for undocumented workers without a driver's license. Farmers who use the H-2A work visa are still required to provide strictly monitored accommodation. Some grumble that employers in other industries such as food service or construction are not required to provide accommodation – fast food workers, migrants or not, can sleep in cardboard boxes in the street, in the snow, without consequence to their employers.

Publicity = Inspections

Over the years occasional media attention to Black Dirt farmers, such as a New York Times story about an innovative farming family, would prompt a flurry of inspections, either from the Department of Labor looking into workers' conditions, from Immigration and Customs Enforcement (ICE) , from legal services officials and even the Internal Revenue Service (IRS). Consequently, growers in the Black Dirt (and in upstate farm regions, as Tom Rivers reports in his book *Farm Hands,*) are extremely publicity shy. A number of farmers did not want to be interviewed for this book. Gratitude goes to those who did contribute their stories and experience, in spite of the heightened rate of inspections that might follow publication.

As well as the many regulations that protect farm workers, they are also provided some special services. One is state-funded child care, called Agri-Business Child Development (ABCD) which cares for migrant farm workers children and other "income eligible" children aged from eight weeks to five years old.

Farm workers are also provided free legal help by the federally funded Legal Services Corporation (LSC) in matters ranging from suspected infringements of the regulations governing work and housing conditions, or wages and employment contracts. Farm workers are also entitled to call on the state funded Farm Worker Legal Services of New York (http://flsny.org) in non-employer related matters such as in-family domestic violence and driving without a license, which are common problems.

It's appropriate that poor, vulnerable people who have been abused in the past should have legal aid. However, the legal services protecting farm workers have been abused – not by workers as much as legal aid lawyers. Many farmers across the United States – including conscientious, law abiding farmers – consider the Legal Services Corporation for farm workers as harassment. In her book *Harvest of Injustice: Legal Services vs. The Farmer,* (1996), Dr. Rael Jean Isaac wrote about small family farmers who were bankrupted and even driven to suicide by legal aid attorneys. Funded by the LSC they would bring suits against farmers who used H-2A work visas. Many farmers, unable to afford legal fees, would settle. A high proportion of these suits were intended to discourage farmers from hiring migrant workers because they would be hard to unionize

Bipartisan criticism of Legal Services activities in the agricultural sector (mainly in the South and on the West Coast) has led to several congressional investigations. An institution designed to help provide legal services to all categories of the poor, Dr. Isaac's book reveals how the LSC's main focus became farms where workers had H-2A visas.

Several times Black Dirt farmers' exasperation with Legal Services attorneys has become confrontational. In one notorious incident in 1987 two farm-owner brothers took their anger out on three female Legal Services lawyers who arrived unannounced on their farm. (One of the lawyers said that they came in response to a call for legal help from farm workers on site). As the New York Times reported it, the brothers "pinned them in their car with trucks, slashed their tires and smashed their windows."

The highly publicized incident aroused conflicting views. While unscheduled visits by Legal Services are unpopular and controversial, the conduct of the farm owners was considered an anomaly, an embarrassment in this normally civil, socially conservative community.

Power Shifts to Workers

No one can dispute that the new dynamics in the farm labor market have shifted the balance of power. As the shortage of farm workers has created greater demand, the farm workers' vulnerability has diminished. Growers are highly motivated to create safe, comfortable conditions, a dignified work environment and fair pay. The Black Dirt growers are not only competing with each other for farm workers, they are in strong competition with other farming regions in the United States. "Farm workers won't come back here if they are badly treated and under-paid," said Stash Grajewski at the farm workers center. Unhappy farm workers abandoning the job mid-season, before harvesting for example, can be ruinous for a farmer.

So, even those hostile to employer-farmers have to recognize that right now, in the Black Dirt, and in most of New York State, the problem for migrant workers is not exploitive or abusive growers. It is the federal immigration law and its enforcement which requires farm workers to live in the shadows, or prohibits them from entering the U.S. legally – therefore more safely – and then leaving to go home to their families so they can return the following season.

Michael Sweeton, current Warwick Town Supervisor, a Republican who, as the owner of The General's Garden nursery, is a grower himself, called the immigration situation "very cruel." He knew of a migrant who worked in the region but had not been able to return home to see his family for eight years for fear he would not get back across the border. "It's not just cruel. It is embarrassing."

Many agricultural workers circulate around the U.S., from farms in California, then on to Florida or Georgia and back to New York in the spring. Some return to the same Black Dirt farms year after year – "recidivists" they are called. Leonard DeBuck of DeBuck Sod farms, had five or six brothers returning to work for him year after year. Vegetable farmer Joe Morgiewicz of Morgiewicz Farms said "I speak for 85% of farmers when I say we treat our workers as family – we can't exist without them." His basic work crew has returned to work on the farm for more than 15 years.

Times have changed since the first farmer settlers came to the United States and did the field work themselves, with their families. Occasionally children still work alongside their parents, learning the protocols of successful farming, helping to pick or sell at markets. (Child Labor laws do not apply to the family of the farm owner.) However, children today are more likely to be at Little League games or engaged in after-school programs than working in the fields. It is very rare to see an American of European heritage, whether child or adult, whether descendants of early settlers or newcomers, laboring in the Black Dirt fields.

First Migrant Workers – POW's

Local Historian and onion farmer John Ruszkiewicz says that among the early foreign hands working the fields were German prisoners of war, brought here in about 1944 when the War Office realized it was cheaper and safer to feed the POW's on American soil than to ship food across the Atlantic to feed them. They were housed at Camp La Guardia in nearby Chester, NY, and other locations, and were paid for their labor.

But even before the German POW's, farm workers were brought in from outside the region when local men left the Black Dirt farms to fight in World War II and women weren't strong enough to lift heavy crates. The first newcomers were African Americans from the South, brought to the region by legendary onion farmer Vincent Kosuga and housed in barracks near Transport Lane beside the Mission Land tract. Members of the Warwick community, including a group of nuns, priests, doctors, teachers and farmers, recognized the dire need for medical services for these farm workers and began to provide them with transport and treatment.

Their numbers and medical needs grew, so in 1959 the ecumenical group of Good Samaritans formally established the Warwick Council of Churches. It eventually became the Warwick Area Migrant Committee. A local settler farm family donated a building on Pulaski Highway, which became the Farmworkers Community Center, now known as Alamo. Here medical, dental and other services have been provided for migrant farm workers and their families for over 30 years. It has offered a safe venue for social gatherings, English as second language instruction, drug and alcohol counseling, a food pantry, farm employment assistance, teen counseling, homework assistance for children, and more.

The original African American farm workers in the Black Dirt eventually moved on to other jobs, their places in the fields taken over in the 1960s by Puerto Ricans, then by Filipinos, followed by groups from Central America and Mexico. Today, the Orange County Farm Bureau estimates that 60% of the farm workers are Mexican. Others are from Jamaica, Honduras, El Salvador, Haiti and other countries in the region.

Because of the large number of Mexican farm workers who frequented the center the building became known as Alamo. Stash Grajewski, the executive director for almost 35 years, had once visited the historic Mexican fort and knew what it looked like. He installed black wrought-iron Mexican-style grilles on the windows so the center actually resembles Alamo.

When New York State budget cuts in 2011 severed all state funding for Alamo its survival was at stake. The community center was saved by Hudson River HealthCare (HRHC), a non-profit Hudson Valley-based healthcare provider, which runs the dental and general health clinic on the site. (The clinic is open to anyone in the community, not just farm workers, and patients pay on a sliding scale based on means.) HRHC's takeover kept the farm worker center operating and modernized the operations. Grajewski estimates that Alamo serves about 2,500 farm workers a year, most of whom make multiple visits.

To the extent that Alamo serves farm workers, improves their quality of life, health, happiness and keeps them content to work in the region, it benefits the growers and has the support of many farmers.

However, the near-religious conviction persists in some quarters that all farmers are worker-abusers, who pay pitiful wages so they can pocket huge profits. These groups have lobbied for agricultural workers to be unionized, and to have the rights and protections the law affords most other categories of work, even when the farm work is seasonal, sometimes just a few weeks a year.

Farmworker Bill

There has been a strong lobby in the New York State Legislature for the Farmworker Fair Labor Practices Act, some of whose provisions farmers say would wipe them off the Black Dirt as fast as another flood from the Wallkill River. Provisions would initiate collective bargaining and overtime pay. Some parts of the bill, such as a minimum wage and a day off every week, are not controversial, since most workers are already paid above minimum wage, and farmers said a day off is standard on most farms – though sometimes it happens according to the rainfall, not the day of the week. The bill passed in the state assembly, but has so far been stalled in the New York senate. That might change in 2016.

Farm workers in every state in the U.S. are specifically exempted from state and federal labor laws. Only California requires that they get overtime pay. There, farms are larger, and the season runs year-round. In New York, and particularly on the small produce farms of the muck lands, there is a brief window – sometimes several weeks, working dawn to dusk - in which to sow and then later to harvest crops. Overtime pay would break many farmers. To avoid it, they would try to hire more workers for shorter periods.

If farm workers are even aware of the proposed bill, they do not support it, says Grajewski at the farm workers' center. "They have nothing to gain from farmers going out of business or cutting their working hours."

Farmworker Hortensia deLeon, works in both the Black Dirt fields and the packing plant for grower John Glebocki, a grower of carrots, scallions, beets and other crops. She said she didn't know about the bill but was opposed to anything that would cut down the hours she could work. An ebullient woman of 51, she said she worked from about 7 am to 6 pm on busy days, earning an average $9 an hour. "I love working outside," she smiled. "I have no complaints."

Gerardo Luna and his wife Lidia Valle were eating lunch during a break from farm work the spring day in 2014 when they were asked their view of the proposed farm bill. Neither had heard of it, but Lidia said that farm work was so hard the overtime pay could be a benefit. But since they, like other farm workers in the region, have no work during the coldest winter months, they preferred to work longer shifts during the farming season. If farmers cut hours to avoid overtime costs they would all suffer, she said.

"The bill is no good for anyone," says Paul Ruszkiewicz. "It's true that farmers will cut hours and that hurts workers who want to maximize work time." Those farmers who can pay overtime will have to increase their prices, making them uncompetitive with farmers growing the same produce in nearby states, none of which require overtime pay.

Farmer Joe Morgiewicz who, with brothers Dave and Dan, supplies about 10 farmers' markets throughout New York and Westchester County, said that "because we deal with fresh food that must be picked daily our labor costs are high. Overtime pay would increase our labor costs by about 30%. There's no way we could afford it," he said. "Yes, we would like to pay them more. But we don't get that kind of return on our product. People (promoting the Bill) have no clue how this business works."

Cheryl Rogowski of Rogowski Farms, and a farm worker advocate, asks "Where will the money come from? Farmers are paid today what they got 10 years ago. At the heart of the matter for farm workers is paying farmers what their food is worth."

In June, 2014, in anticipation of the Bill being reintroduced, State Assemblyman James Skoufis (D-Woodbury), organized a tour of the region for a group of members of the New York Legislature who were concerned about what they been told of conditions for farm workers. They visited Alamo, and toured several produce farms, where they saw farm conditions up close.

Onion Farmer Chris Pawelski, who was along on the tour, said that some of the tour participants were totally unaware of what was provided to farm workers. "Some came with preconceptions because when they learned about all the services, programs and protections available free to farm workers, their jaws dropped."

The Minister

Among those pushing for passage of the Farmworker Fair Labor Practices Act is an Episcopal minister, Reverend Richard Witt, who runs the Rural Migrant Ministry in Poughkeepsie, New York. For more than 25 years Rev.

Witt has led a spirited campaign for farm workers' rights, based largely on public humiliation of farmers. (Those who work for religious institutions like his are exempt from the very same Labor Law provisions as are farm workers, including overtime pay.)

Sister Pam Wagner and Sister Fran Liston of The Mustard Seed Migrant Ministry in the Black Dirt region, the nuns who deal daily with farm worker issues as they care for the field workers' children, say the Rural Migrant Ministry did intend to help migrant workers. But the message that the Rev. Witt put out – that all farmers were abusive – was a form of "dualistic thinking that is harmful. It's not our experience with farmers. Nor is it what we have heard from farm workers themselves. We know of farmers treating workers with generosity and compassion – instances, for example, when farmers paid for their workers to return home to their home country when there was a family crisis."

Local farmers were angered by a TV documentary aired by Regional News Network in 1996 in which the Reverend Witt told a story about a farm worker's 6-year-old child who was killed in a road accident. Witt claimed on TV that the child was struck by a car at night. He then described how farm workers who needed to use the toilet at night were forced to run across a busy highway in the dark. The toilet had no door and faced the road, he said, implying that was why the child was hit by a car in the dark. Then Witt alleged that at a memorial service organized by his rural ministry for the dead child, a farm crop duster buzzed the grieving family.

Farmer Alex Kocot, whose right-hand man on his farm was the dead child's father, said that the Reverend Witt's account was fiction. Kocot said: "The child was riding a bicycle with his brother in broad daylight, heading towards a friend's home up Pulaski Highway. The boys crossed the road without looking behind them and were hit by a car driven by a young woman. The older boy flew into the air and landed on the car and was killed." Kocot's family attended the funeral with the grieving parents.

As for the toilet, which played no role in the child's death, Kocot said it was on the same side of the highway as the workers' housing. "If there actually was a memorial service organized by the rural ministry, farming would have continued in the neighboring farms. That story about the crop duster buzzing them…its crap. He makes this stuff up."

A respected executive of a prominent Hudson Valley non-profit who works with farm workers in the region knew both the family of the young boy who was killed, and the circumstances of the accident. The executive said the Reverend Witt had changed the story in order to create antagonism to farmers. "There are well intentioned advocacy groups who are not always truthful. It's too bad because the best way to protect the farm workers is to work with farmers, not stigmatize them."

Questions sent twice to the Rural Migrant Ministry about Black Dirt growers' treatment of their farm workers, and Rev Witt's account in the TV documentary, were ignored.

(There are other concerned groups lobbying for better pay and conditions for farm workers and all those employed in food service. Among the groups are the Food Chain Workers Alliance, the U.S. Food Sovereignty Alliance, the Rural Coalition, and the Student/Farmworker Alliance.)

Supermarkets

The issue of farm worker abuse and pay nationwide got more nationwide attention at the end of 2014 when American actress, activist and producer Eva Longoria began promoting Sanjay Rawal's film Food Chains which she co-produced. Rawal's documentary is about the Coalition of Immokalee Workers in Florida State whose protests changed the working conditions and pay on tomato farms.

After a preview of his film in New York City Rawal said that the culprits in the question of farm worker pay were not the farmers as much as the retail chains, the supermarkets and stores like Walmart which pay low prices for produce. "Paying just one cent more would dramatically improve farm worker pay.

"While the villain of the past has been the government, Jim Crow, or farmers themselves, the enemy of the farm worker these days is the friend of every middle class family in America. The companies with the largest purchasing power, namely supermarkets, control our modern food system," said Rawal.

Supermarkets have slim profit margins, and are valued amenities in communities where they exist. (Indeed, the Shoprite Supermarket near the Black Dirt valley has started making a major feature of its range of fresh "local" produce from Gurda Farms nearby.) But by shifting the emphasis to more equitable payment to farmers and farm workers, and away from demonizing growers, specially struggling small family growers, Rawal might be doing farmers and their workers a favor.

A "Recidivist"

In drenching rain one September day – peak harvest time for many farms – workers were picking and packing before the ferocious winds predicted later in the afternoon. Every hour counts when crops are ripe and extreme weather is on the way. These Black Dirt fields were at picking perfection when they were utterly wiped out by the weather catastrophe in 2011, costing the region's farmers and their farm workers incalculable losses.

At the Alamo Mario Fernandez, the Guatamalan-born outreach worker who is director Stash Grajewski's right hand man, was busy fielding a staccato of phone calls from people asking for workers for various jobs, farm and non-farm, troubleshooting farm worker issues and giving advice, most of it in Spanish. The only migrant in the Alamo was a Latino woman, a worker-turned-farmer, accompanied by her Mexican male farm worker. There is a small but growing number of migrant workers who have rented or bought farm land and are now hiring migrant workers themselves, just as the Poles who first worked in the region as sharecroppers went on to buy their own farms.

Obviously farm workers, like farmers, are individuals, with their own rich histories, skills, experiences and stories. It was important to talk to one. Fernandez (known to everyone as Mario), an efficient, amiable young man who speaks good English, suggested Juan Mendoza. A farm worker from Leon Guanajuato, in the South of Mexico, Mendoza had been returning to the Black Dirt as a seasonal worker for 24 years. At the time he was working at Dagele Bros. Produce Farm, where the three brothers grow a variety of crops. Their biggest categories are onions and lettuce.

Mario drove a quarter mile from the Alamo to the Dagele farm lettuce workers' quarters, a single story building set beside the fields where the muck soil meets the uplands. Mendoza emerged, a shy man, about 5'8" and stocky. In the spacious kitchen and communal dining area was a table facing large windows overlooking the lettuce fields. A seasonal farm worker in the U.S. since 1979, when he was 16, Mendoza crisscrossed between grape and fruit farms in California and Florida for seven years before he first came to Orange County to harvest lettuce in 1986.

As a master of lettuce picking, with the particular, prized skills required for harvesting this fragile crop, he estimated his hourly income at $15– almost double the minimum wage at the time. The lettuce harvesters, Mendoza explained, are paid by the piece, not the hour. "We get $1 a crate, and on good days we can do 20-30 crates an hour. It depends on how clean the lettuce is and how much of the leaf is old and has to be removed. That slows you down."

His equipment was a sharp knife with an 11 inch blade. He moved swiftly through the fields decapitating the plant at a precise point below the head, and then slashing off the discolored leaves before packing them. On busy harvest days, Mendoza said, his team of 15 workers at Dagele farms packed over 2,000 boxes of lettuce for market. He was proud of this number, repeating it as an accomplishment, a testament to their productivity (certainly not as a complaint about hard labor).

The pay was better in the Black Dirt region, said Mendoza, but the conditions in the fields were often tougher than they are in the state of Florida; the dark soil held so much moisture that the heat and humidity could be uncomfortable. On days when the humidity and heat were most intense some Black Dirt farmers allowed workers to leave for lunch at noon and return to finish harvesting in the late afternoon, when conditions were cooler. The rule on some farms was that if temperatures rose above 95 F workers went home for the day.

Mendoza's crew live, work and relax together and, he said, they became more than a team, they were like family. His own family – his wife Maya and five children – lived in Mexico. He went home twice a year but that year his 20-year-old son Juan Jr., was with him at the Dagele's farm. Mendoza gave up his spot on the lettuce harvesting team so his son could take his place. Instead, the father undertook to be the cook in the team quarters, paid by the whole crew. "I hate it," he said in English. "Too much work!" He grumbled that the team made a mess in the kitchen and he really didn't enjoy cooking.

The accommodation, provided rent-free by the Dagele farm, had two dormitory rooms limited to eight men each, with three showers and three toilets – all in compliance with the strict regulations governing worker housing. The crew leader had a separate room adjacent to their quarters. By comparison, when Mendoza goes to Florida State to harvest lettuce later in the year he will share an apartment with a group of other farm workers and they will pay rent. "This is good," he said, looking at the large, amply equipped kitchen. "And no rent."

Asked about a provision of the proposed New York State Farmworker Fair Labor Practices Act, that farm workers must get overtime pay, Mendoza said that he sometimes works a 13-hour day. But he did not endorse legally required overtime. "Piece work is better for us. " He did approve of one element of that would-be Labor Practices Act: a day off every week for farm workers. "Sometime we work seven days a week, and sometimes we work just a few hours on Sunday. I would like a full day off. One day to rest, do business, do laundry."

When the workers return from the fields in the evening they shower, have dinner and "a few beers" and go to sleep. There are reports that sometimes farm workers carouse to excess. Mendoza smiled. "Too tired." But later he admitted that some of the guys get drunk from time to time. If they keep the other workers awake, the crew leader throws them out. There were no drugs at all, he said, looking very disapproving.

Inspectors from the various New York State authorities with oversight over farm workers' conditions come to the premises about three times during the picking season, Mendoza said. They make a number of required checks, such as the number of occupants, the number of showers and toilets per occupant, basic hygiene and the presence of smoke alarms and fire extinguishers. Everything was fine at Dagele's farm, Mendoza said. He was asked what happens if inspectors find a problem. "The farmer fixes it," he said.

In spite of his aversion to cooking, Mendoza seemed enthusiastic when asked what he prepared for the team. Bags of red and green chili peppers, limes, sweet potatoes and a huge carton of tortillas were produced. He pointed outside to the BBQ, where he grilled steaks and ribs, their favorite meals.

He would do this job for just a few more weeks. When the season was over in the Black Dirt, in early October, he would return to Mexico to see his family. "Its not rest," he sighed. "It's hard work fixing the house."

A gentle-mannered man, the only time he was effusive was when describing something he experienced in the state of Florida: harassment by the police. "I think they hate every man with dark skin." He added that life was made additionally difficult because farm workers were frequently victims of crime. The problem was exacerbated when the police, to whom victims must turn, are hostile to migrants – which makes them more attractive targets for criminals.

How do conditions here in the Black Dirt region of New York compare? Mendoza said the police in this region do not harass migrant workers, and there is no crime problem – a fact confirmed by current Warwick Town Supervisor Michael Sweeton. He was asked Mendoza if he was treated with respect in this community. "Yes, yes," he replied, nodding.

If he moved his family from Mexico to the United States, he said, he would like to settle them here, in the Black Dirt. But that's some time in the future. In the meantime, he had to continue his annual migration – home to Mexico, then back to Florida. And the following June, he planned to head back north to help harvest in the Black Dirt fields – a true "recidivist." ■

Onion Thrips, *Thrips tabaco*, Lindemann, 1889

CHAPTER 8: PESTICIDES, POLLUTION, PARANOIA, AND FEEDING THE POOR

"Rules on getting the pesticide license are more stringent than getting a driver's license."

So rigid are the rules governing the use of pesticides in the Black Dirt (and all of New York State for that matter), and so pricey are the chemical brews that kill bugs, weeds and plant diseases, you might wonder why all muck land farmers haven't decided to go organic. The fact is that the wonderful qualities that make the black soil so productive – fertility, water retention, soil warmth, high sulfur content – also make it the Waldorf Astoria for weeds.

Edward Smith, author of *The Vegetable Gardener's Bible* and *The Vegetable Gardener's Container Bible* estimates that there are something like 5,000 weed seeds in every cubic inch of soil. Iowa State University Agronomy Department has a weed history website which estimates that "in disturbed habitats, such as farm fields, the weed seed bank can range from 200 to 54,000 seeds per cubic foot."

So its not surprising that being organic in the Black Dirt is highly labor intensive. Humans must do much of the weeding that conventional farmers do with chemicals. And the organic pesticides used to control bugs and diseases are less effective than those used by conventional growers. This all makes organic farming more expensive, with lower yields.

Soils in other regions, particularly the Southwest, with its dry conditions, are far more friendly to organic farming – a choice many farmers make in those regions. There is only one "Certified Organic" farm in the Black Dirt. However, a growing number use "pesticide free" farm practices and, according to Maire Ullrich of the CCE, the overwhelming trend among farmers in the region is towards more "natural" methods. Increasingly, conventional farmers use the same pesticides as organic farmers – or variations of them. For example, Spintor, an effective conventional pesticide, is a variation of Entrust, used by organic farmers, both derived from a natural ingredient *Spinosad*.

A new invasive pest called *swede midge* recently started to attack Brassilica crops (including cabbage, broccoli, cauliflower, kale, Brussels sprouts, collard greens, savoy and kohlrabi) in the Northeast. Conventional farmers have been able to control the pest but it has been devastating to small organic farms because so far there is no known effective "organic" control.

Ullrich, one of the most knowledgeable people in the region on the question of pesticides and their use, says "New York State has what are probably the most stringent laws governing pesticides in the United Sates." (Pesticide is an overall term, covering a range of killing or repelling substances, including insecticides, herbicides, fungicides, and bactericides.)

Slight pesticide residues do sometimes remain on vegetables and fruits – even though in amounts so minute they are considered completely safe by the regulatory agencies. But any amount of residue concerns many consumers. The effect of pesticides on water, insects and wildlife consequent to conventional farming also worries environmentalists and all those who care about sustainability in farming.

Ullrich points out that use of pesticides is not only regulated by the state, but also by the U.S. Department of Environmental Conservation and the Environmental Protection Agency, both institutions that are concerned about pesticides' effects on the soil, water, insects and wildlife.

Farmers must have a pesticide applicator's license before they can acquire most pesticides. The license can only be obtained after education at a certified seminar, followed by exams. That license has to be renewed every five years by recertification, which can only follow renewed education and further exams. "The rules on getting the pesticide license are more stringent than getting a drivers' license," says Ullrich, who knows well. She conducts the seminars and exams herself. If farmers fail they must be retested until they pass, or they won't get a license.

Modern farmers have to be extremely savvy on the issue. Cornell University's New York State Integrated Pest Management Program website has a formula for determining the Environment Impact Quotient (EIQ) of individual pesticides. It shows how complicated, but thorough, is the regime – and how much consideration goes into the impact on the world around the plant being treated.

$$EIQ = \{C[(DT*5)+(DT*P)]+[(C*((S+P)/2)*SY)+(L)]+[(F*R)+ (D*((S+P)/2)*3)+(Z*P*3)+(B*P*5)]\}/3$$

DT = dermal toxicity, C = chronic toxicity, SY = systemicity, F = fish toxicity, L = leaching potential, R = surface loss potential, D = bird toxicity, S = soil half-life, Z = bee toxicity, B = beneficial arthropod toxicity, P = plant surface half-life.

The pesticide brew that a farmer applies will depend on what he/she is trying to kill, and how prevalent that problem is at that time: a mild infestation of onion maggots would require a different concoction than a severe attack of thrips. In the case of onions, the biggest threat is a fungus. A fungicide will be mixed with a surfactant to coat the waxy leaves and prevent runoff, and a protectant is added to provide a barrier to fungi.

Each crop has its own range of threats. "Farmers get lots of advice from me, as well as from the chemical companies that sell the pesticides, on what and how much to put in the brew. Pesticides and fertilizers are extremely expensive and no one wants to use any more than absolutely necessary," says Ullrich. Like modern drugs for humans, the newer and more effective the pesticide, the more it costs. The older ones that have gone off patent are the cheapest.

Reading the list of pesticides available, it is interesting how many have been given appealing, encouraging, non-toxic sounding names. There's Liberty, Inspire, Fascination, Acclaim Super, Excell Super and Prestige. Suggesting a war between man and bugs, many insecticides are pugilistic sounding brews – Sniper, Matador, Avenge, Vanguard, Warrior, Ambush, Marksman and Pounce, to name a few. To make farmers feel like noble cowboys on the range are concoctions named Crossbow and Lasso and, of course, the ubiquitous Round-Up.

Climate Change

Ullrich warns that some of the traditional and time-tried farming practices in the Black Dirt are now being challenged by climate change. "We are seeing diseases and bugs never found here before. We are finding some that occur all year down south, but are normally killed off here by the winter. Now they are surviving."

Climate change is credited for the Late Blight, a fungal disease that attacked tomatoes and potatoes in the northeast in 2009. "I've never seen anything like it in my 25 years in the business. And then the stinkbug arrived. It's a national problem," she revealed.

Environmentalists in the region have concerns about the effect of chemical residues polluting the water that runs off the Black Dirt farms into the Wallkill River and its creeks. One old study of the water in the Wallkill showed that it was cleaner after coursing ten miles through the muck land than when it entered at the New Jersey border, where pollution from domestic and commercial development is evident.

Newer studies show there is some pollution in the Wallkill River as it leaves the muck lands but it's scientifically difficult to apportion responsibility - how much is pesticide from farms, or the wide range of toxins that run into the river after it originates upstream in New Jersey? Some chemicals that haven't been used for over 40 years, such as DDT, have such a long life they are still found in samples and will be present for years to come.

State laws governing pesticides include requirements that farmers provide officials information on where they store their pesticide supplies (not in the kitchen!), and that they carefully log how much they apply. They must also follow strict guidelines on how long their fields must be quarantined after application, what contact farm workers can have with the chemicals and the warning signs that must be displayed. For example, "Don't Approach!" worst-case warnings are for 12 – 24 hours after spraying for organic farms, and up to five days for conventional pesticides.

Strict regulations are justified: pesticides can lead to a wide range of problems in humans including skin irritation, nausea, asthma, learning disabilities, birth defects, reproductive dysfunction, diabetes, Parkinson's, Alzheimer's and a wide range of cancers. Many are so toxic that a third of all suicides, mostly in the developing world, are committed by people who deliberately consumed a pesticide.

Many non-farming residents of the Black Dirt valley become alarmed every summer when the sky is filled with the whines and drones of the aerial crop sprayer as it swoops over the muck lands dropping clouds of diluted pesticides. There is widespread suspicion that aerial spraying fills the atmosphere with poison. Ullrich is adamant that the aerial spraying is also subject to the most stringent safety and environmental impact regulations. By law, the pesticide is diluted with an anti- dispersant so it doesn't drift. Many of the crops with vines, such as pumpkins or zucchini, are treated by a crop sprayer from the air because using a ground vehicle or treating plants on foot would damage the plant tendrils or vines spreading across the ground.

Ullrich dismisses rumors that there have been "cancer pockets"–unusually high incidents of cancer in a small region of the Black Dirt– that can be attributed to pesticide use. She believes any such incidents might be attributed to genetics since families in the region tend to be extended. However, there are two types of cancer prevalent among farmers everywhere that are work related – skin and lung. Being out in the sun unprotected by sunblock, and being free of workplace restrictions on smoking takes a toll on the nation's farming community. "That said, farmers do use chemicals that can be harmful if you don't know they have been applied. The public shouldn't just meander onto a farm anywhere, just as you can't walk into a factory. Apart from being an insurance nightmare, farming can be dangerous."

As the person who is frequently called on to give a chemical prescription for an ailing crop, no one knows more than Ullrich about the hazards. She is convinced that properly used pesticides are safe and appropriate. "In 1950 a United States farmer produced food to feed 23 people a year. That figure now is 155 people. That is thanks in part to the chemicals we use to kill bugs, weeds and diseases," she says.

"People need to comprehend how much pesticides help to put food on the table, here and worldwide. With limited arable land we have vastly expanded the pounds of produce per acre. Better food has helped to double our life expectancy in 100 years. Antibiotics also play a role in our new longevity. Admittedly, antibiotics can lead to resistance. There are problems.

But no one suggests humans simply ban antibiotics."

Organic

However, the market for organic food has continued to rise steadily in the United States at a rate of about 9.4 percent a year, with the fruit and vegetable category contributing close to 50 percent of those new dollars. Organic food sales now represent 4.2 percent of all U.S. food sales, up from 4 percent in 2010, according to the Organic Trade Association.

The International Federation of Organic Movements defines organic agriculture as "a production system that sustains the health of soils, ecosystems and people. It relies on ecological processes, biodiversity and cycles adapted to local conditions, rather than the use of inputs with adverse effects. Organic agriculture combines tradition, innovation and science to benefit the shared environment and promote fair relationships and a good quality of life for all involved."

In other words, organic foods are produced using methods that do not involve modern synthetic pesticides and chemical fertilizers. The United States, Canada, Japan and many other countries require producers to obtain special certifications in order to market food as "organic." Locally, certification is provided by the Northeast Organic Farming Association of New York (NOFANY) which does repeated onsite inspections and tests and requires considerable paperwork. It also lists all the Certified Organic farmers by county.

As previously described, the warm, moist, rich Black Dirt soil is less suitable for organic farming than is the soil in almost all other agricultural regions of the U.S..

A growing number of Black Dirt farmers, including Jeff and Adina Bialis of J & A Farms, use organic practices but don't have the official verification as organic. J & A Farms are "Certified Naturally Grown," an alternative to organic, and have adopted the "Farmer's Pledge," which is also regulated and certified by NOFANY.

Farmers whose primary distribution outlet for their produce is the farmers' markets in urban areas – especially New York City and its boroughs – report that consumers commonly ask if the produce they sell is organic. "Sometimes they walk away if you say it isn't," says John Madura of Madura Farms on the Mission Land tract. Those tending the stands in the city Greenmarkets, including Alex Paffenroth of Paffenroth Gardens and his daughter Deanne, spend some time explaining that their practices, while not "certified" organic, are still healthy and minimize pesticide use.

Joe Morgiewicz whose family farm supplies 35 varieties of vegetables and herbs at ten farmers markets in the New York region, says frequently customers with a prejudice in favor of organic farming ask him where and how he grows his produce. "Sometimes I tell them things they didn't know which changes their minds – such as pesticides are used in organic farming, and that because they are not as effective as conventional pesticides, multiple applications are sometimes required."

"I hate pesticides with a passion," says Alex Kocot, whose 400 acre farm includes 170 acres of onions. "But people believe organic means no pesticides at all. In fact they often have to spray more often. If I was organic I'd only be able to grow 30 acres of onions, not 170. This soil is a hotbed for weeds and even though we spray, we still have to do hand weeding throughout the season."

An exception is Jeff and Adina Bialis of J & A Farm who report that applying strictly organic farming practices of the kind that were used before modern pesticides were even invented, they have been able to almost eradicate weeds on their 12 acres and achieve yields commensurate with conventional farmers.

Because the organic method requires more human labor, the pesticide brews to kill bugs and diseases are sometimes pricey but less effective, and production is usually lower, organically grown produce almost always costs more – from 10% to 100% more than conventionally grown. It is harder for organic farms to turn a profit.

However, the number of organic farms in the Black Dirt is growing. The Chester Agricultural Center, LLC, a group of investors committed to making land affordable and accessible to experienced farmers, plans to acquire up to 270 acres in the Black Dirt near the town of Chester and lease it to farmers specifically for organic farming. Among the investors is the Ralph E. Ogden Foundation in Mountainville whose aim is to conserve farmland and encourage organic farming. A group of farmers have already leased a 30-acre parcel and plan to grow organic vegetables for restaurants in New York City.

A powerful new incentive to grow organic soon arrives right next to the Black Dirt when Amy's Kitchen, an organic and natural food processing company that sells in all the major food outlets throughout the U.S., builds its new $100-million facility beside the Wallkill River in Goshen, the Orange County seat. Construction on the 580,000 square foot plant is expected to start in 2016.

Even as the organic movement grows, many scientists as well as regular consumers, ask if buying organic is worth the extra cost. In September 2012 a large-scale study from Stanford University found that when it comes to nutrition, organic foods, such as meat, dairy, and produce, may not be worth the extra cash. Researchers said organic foods were no healthier and not significantly safer than conventional foods and produce grown with pesticides.

Most consumers pay more for organically grown produce in the hope they are purchasing healthier, more nutrient-dense food. However, Stanford researcher Dena Bravata said: "There isn't much difference between organic and conventional foods, if you're an adult and making a decision based-solely on your health." After reviewing thousands of papers, the Stanford researchers found that there was also no guarantee organic food would be pesticide-free. But it did have 30 percent lower levels compared to conventional products. The researchers found that the pesticide levels of all foods generally fell within the allowable safety limits.

Maire Ullrich expressed concern that the Stanford University report was a "meta-study that contradicted within itself whether organic was better or not." The proponents of organic foods point out that the study mainly addressed nutrition comparisons, not short or long term health issues, or the impact of organic production versus conventional on the environment. Nor did the study address taste. (It's hard to find scientific evidence that organic food tastes better. Blind taste tests have been inconclusive: results tend to confirm the convictions of the taster.)

In a New York Times essay titled "Food for the Wealthy, not the Poor" Bjorn Lomborg, the author of *The Skeptical Environmentalist* (2001) and director of Copenhagen Consensus Center argues that the higher cost of organic food has serious negative health consequences. "Eating more fruits and vegetables is incredibly more important than avoiding already well-regulated pesticides." He argues that, using World Cancer Research Fund data, "a decrease of just 10 percent in fruit and vegetable consumption in the U.S. because of higher prices would cause an increase in cancer of about 4.6 percent of the total number of cancers, or some 26,000 additional cancer deaths annually." (Lomborg was ranked one of the 100 top thinkers of the 20th Century by *Time Magazine*, April 26, 2004.)

Most people prefer organic food because of an aversion to pesticides. However, the majority of organic farms do use pesticides, just not synthetic ones. Some of these natural pesticides, like rotenone and copper sulfate, are designed to kill and have been linked to a variety of diseases. Plenty of what's "natural" is deadly, including arsenic, anthrax and botulinum. Maire Ullrich points out that one of the most dangerous pesticides used by conventional farmers, is a "natural" neurotoxin derived from that favorite fall-blooming plant, the chrysanthemum.

Dr. Henry I. Miller, a physician and molecular biologist, who was the founding director of the FDA's Office of Biotechnology, adds his voice. Writing in the *Wall Street Journal* (May 15, 2014) under the headline "Organic Farming Is Not Sustainable" he argues against every major assumption about the environmental advantages of organic farming, describing its detrimental effects on soil and water and its contribution to carbon emissions.

It is certainly not trendy to smear organic anything in leftist urban circles. But there is some disdain, as expressed by Roger Cohen, Op-Ed contributor to the *New York Times* (September 6, 2012.)

"Organic has long since become an ideology, the romantic back-to-nature obsession of an upper middle class able to afford it and oblivious, in their affluent narcissism, to the challenge of feeding a planet whose population will surge to 9 billion before the middle of the century and whose poor will get a lot more nutrients from the two regular carrots they can buy for the price of one organic carrot. An effective form of premium branding rather than a science, a slogan rather than better nutrition, "organic" has oozed over the menus, markets and malls of the world's upscale neighborhood at a remarkable pace."

If only these issues were clear-cut, good versus bad, beneficial versus detrimental. But complicating our aversion to pesticides – natural or synthetic – and the harm they do to insects, animals, the soil and the water, AND the need to increase productivity at lower cost, is the fact that there is another way: genetically modified organisms, or GMOs. Better known as Frankenfoods, GMOs are the scourge of the organic movement and concern many people. But they can reduce or eradicate the need for some insecticides, herbicides and even some fungicides – and increase the nutritional value of everyday vegetables.

"GMOs have the potential to up crop yields, increase nutrition value, and generally improve farming practices while reducing synthetic chemical use -- which is exactly what organic farming seeks to do," says Christie Wilcox, of the University of Hawaii and a blogger at *Scientific American*. She reports that sweet potatoes are being engineered to be resistant to a virus that currently decimates the African harvest every year, which could feed millions in some of the poorest nations in the world. "Scientists have created carrots high in calcium to fight osteoporosis and tomatoes high in antioxidants."

"In my mind," Wilcox writes, "the ideal future will merge conventional and organic methods, using GMOs and/or other new technologies to reduce pesticide use while increasing the bioavailability of soils, crop yield, nutritional quality and biodiversity in agricultural lands. New technology isn't the enemy of organic farming; it should be its strongest ally."

But consumer antipathy to GMO foods is strong. In a *New York Times* poll in early 2013, about half the respondents said that, given a choice, they would not eat GM vegetables, fruits and grains. Americans overwhelmingly support labeling foods that have been genetically modified or engineered. Three-quarters of the poll respondents expressed concern about such products in their food, with most of them worried about the health effects. More than a third of those who worried about GMOs said they fear that these foods cause cancer or allergies. About a quarter of them believe GMOs are toxic.

It could be that the word GMO has become associated with the name Monsanto, a giant U.S. chemical company producing GMO products, whose patent protection and other practices have made it one of the most loathed companies in the food world, even though GMO seeds and products are now produced by scores of other companies worldwide.

New York food writer Mark Bittman, noting that the FDA had declared new breeds of GM potato and apple to be safe, wrote in the New York Times (March 25, 2015): "In fact, to date, there's little credible evidence that any food grown with genetic engineering techniques is dangerous to human health – unless, like corn and soybeans, it's turned into junk food."

Hundreds of scientific studies have been performed over recent decades to determine the impact of GM crops or plants on human and animal health. A list with over 400 articles can be found at the site of Biology Fortified, an independent, nonprofit organization. In 2013 the UK environmental secretary Owen Patterson became one of the most outspoken of prominent Europeans in support of GM crops.

Maire Ullrich believes that consumers are confused about the whole issue. As an example, she notes that in a recent study 80 percent of respondents claimed that they never eat any DNA – even though it it is present in every organism, every morsel of plant or animal food we ever consume.

"Why are consumers so wary of the GMO in agriculture but totally accepting of the GMO in medicine?" She points out that billions of people are taking medicines that are the product of GMOs, including insulin. Other diseases being treated with medications that are the result of genetic engineering are hemophilia, hepatitis B, heart disease, stroke and a variety of cancers. Hormone treatments, including birth control pills, are the result of medical GMO.

Perhaps one day GMOs that are proven safe might be available for onions, celery, beets, potatoes and all the other crops now grown in the bountiful fields of the Black Dirt. They might enable Black Dirt farmers to greatly reduce or eliminate pesticide use, lower costs, increase profits, pay higher wages and expand the amount of land they farm and crops they grow – at lower cost to consumers! But as long as consumers remain deeply concerned about the science of genetic modification Black Dirt produce farmers will continue to be wary of GMO. The economics of small family farms are complicated enough without creating hostility.

CHAPTER 9: SMALL FARM FINANCES

"They love the land, and they love the job they do.
They are certainly not in it for the money."

Americans enjoy a food supply that is plentiful, affordable and among the world's safest. And yet the small farmers and ranchers who produce most of it receive only 19 cents out of every dollar spent on food at home and away from home. The rest goes to wages, processing, marketing, transportation and distribution.

The signal that something in the market is wrong is that in 1980, farmers and ranchers received 31 cents out of every dollar spent on food. That's about 50% more than they get now, 35 years later, according to the U.S. Farm Bureau.

Some facts from the U.S. Department of Agriculture (USDA):
- 97 percent of the 2.1 million farms in the United States are family-owned operations.
- 88 percent of all U.S. farms are small family farms, meaning they

have a gross cash income of less than $350,000 a year. (An average 89% goes to costs.)

- 42 percent of farmers work a second job to make ends meet, or to acquire medical insurance or other benefits, or only farm as a sideline.
- 14 percent of Family Farm incomes are below the poverty line for a family of four ($24,250).

The U.S. Department of Agriculture predicts that the specialty crop farm businesses – the kind that dominate in the Black Dirt valley - will experience a decrease in average Net Cash Farm Income (NCFI) of 18 percent in 2015, after what was forecast as a nationwide 31 percent drop in 2014. Labor expenses, which make up 40 percent of all cash expenses for specialty crop farms, are forecast to increase 4 percent due to higher wages, and other cash expenses are forecast to rise 6 percent.

As for the profitability of those vast mono-culture farms that have received generous pay-outs for years, there is a little known fact of farm economics: As the *New York Times* reported early in 2014, vastly more money can be made on those farms by growing specialty crops - vegetables and fruit – instead of corn and wheat. This is pertinent when much of that corn goes to produce ethanol for automobiles or to feed cattle, and what corn does feed humans is the high fructose corn sugar that is blamed for obesity and its consequent health horrors, diabetes among them.

An acre of corn was fetching a net average of $284 in the late winter of 2013, while an acre of apples would make $2,000 or more and a sophisticated vegetable farm using high tunnels to increase yield could make $100,000 an acre. Encouraged by the westward spread of the market for fresh, local vegetables some Midwestern farmers were switching from corn to specialty crops. Of course, if they can produce and transport cheaply, and are inclined to truck crops to the east coast, this trend might create more competition for Black Dirt farmers. (At the cost of about $8,000 per tractor-trailer ride from the west coast to the New York region in 2015, trucking was prohibitively pricey.) In any case, for demanding consumers "fresh" and "local" is still a winning issue because of the health and environmental benefits.

When remuneration is the topic, it is relevant to repeat that this is the country where families pay just 10.1 % of disposable income for their food.

Consumers in other countries spend a much higher percentage of their earnings on what they eat. France, 18%; Japan, 26%; Mexico, 33%; and India, 51%. Part of the reason for the low percentage outlay on food in the U.S. is that people earn more here, and thus have more disposable income. But the fact remains that compared to other countries, food is a bargain. Paying less to American farmers leaves fellow citizens with more income for other expenditures. That might be healthcare or education. It also might be new TV's, eating out, second homes, vacations, bigger cars...

Black Dirt farmers, like growers throughout New York State, have in recent years faced a hike in fuel costs, unemployment insurance charges, and increased prices for seeds, pesticides and fertilizer. With rising land values, the New York Farm Bureau appealed to the state to help farmers by putting a cap on property taxes. According to Farm Credit East, farmers in this state pay $26.21/acre in property taxes, which is nearly $20 more than the national average.

So, if growing costs are rising across the board, why don't Black Dirt farmers simply charge more for their produce?

They would, but the "market" price is not set by the farmers themselves. Worse, prices are almost as unpredictable as the weather, which makes planning for forthcoming seasons a gamble. Price uncertainty is particularly pertinent to those growers dependent on wholesale distributors who supply their produce to supermarkets, chain stores and chain restaurants. What these growers are paid is subject to supply and demand, which is now influenced not just by the exigencies of weather, or crop diseases, or the whims of consumers, but also by competition from growers across the United States and the world. It is supply and demand gone global. Drought in the Midwest as much as a tsunami in India affects prices received here in the muck lands of Orange County.

Over the past two decades Black Dirt farmers and their colleagues in the Northeast states have seen increasing competition from other U.S. growers in the Midwest and the West, where the growing seasons are longer, and some of the basic farming costs are lower.

Additionally, competition from overseas is rapidly expanding – from the European Union, Canada, Mexico, Peru, Chile...and the list now includes China, which already exports garlic to California, crushing the garlic farmers in that state.

Between about 1990 and 2006 the share of total U.S. agricultural imports rose from 11.5 percent to 13.3 percent. But now, 15% of all food consumed in the U.S. over a year is imported.

The Economic Research Service of the USDA (2007) reports that the dominant foreign suppliers of fresh vegetables to the U.S. are the North American Free Trade Agreement (NAFTA) countries - Mexico and Canada. The volume and variety of fresh produce imports have allowed U.S. consumers to eat more fruit and vegetables and enjoy year-round access to fresh produce, which is fabulous – but it has wreaked havoc in the lives of some produce farmers in the region, including here in the muck lands.

Small farmers complain they are not on an even playing field: other countries, including those in the European Union and Canada, help to keep their produce prices lower with government subsidies of one kind or another, such as paying part of the transport costs. Some agricultural activist groups in the U.S. oppose that central principal of globalization, international free trade, because of the harm it does to small farmers in America who can't compete with the cheaper (often subsidized) imports. Some of those same activist groups also oppose free trade because of the harm it does to small farmers in other poor countries who can't compete with the (subsidized) mega-farms in America.

"Ironically, the cheaper, imported crops are likely to come from countries with fewer pesticide controls and safety regulations," notes Paul Ruszkiewicz of the Orange County Vegetable Growers' Association. "And to get these potentially unsafe crops to U.S. markets requires transport over longer distances, which means burning more fossil fuels." In recent years the Country of Origin Labeling (COOL) laws required retailers, such as grocery stores, to notify their customers with information regarding the source of certain foods. That law now includes fresh fruit and vegetables. Consumers can avoid produce from countries whose safety standards concern them.

Food supply activists put the blame for the low payments to local growers on agribusinesses, and megastores like Walmart. They claim these omnipotent groups can use their market dominance to control the prices that farmers receive and consumers pay. Most consumers, however, want produce prices kept low – a dilemma for those who want to see small specialty farms thrive and call for farm workers to be paid more.

The large food processors and supermarket chains contend that their size offers consumers more choice and affordability: the economy of scale. Food and Water Watch, a group that advocates against industrialized agriculture, disputes this. They claim that these companies rarely pass their lower costs on to consumers through lower retail prices.

There is also the incontrovertible but dismal fact that many unhealthy, processed and popular foods cost less – sometimes a lot less - than healthy fresh farm produce, with profound effects on the correlation between poverty and obesity, and the consequent rise in healthcare costs in the U.S.. As food writer Michael Pollan famously pointed out in an essay in the *New York Times* (April 27, 2007) 100 calories of Twinkie costs less than 100 calories of carrot because in spite of all the ingredients and processing involved in making a Twinkie, the corn, wheat and soybean that make up the sugar and fat in this sweet, cream-filled high carb cake, all come from those farms that have been recipients of billions of dollars in *federal subsidies*. [Ed. note: Italics added].

The Price of Onions

Ed Sobiech, third generation son of Polish settler farmers and one of the larger Black Dirt onion re-packers and distributors, says the low price paid to onion growers is simply a result of the supply surpassing demand. "Everywhere that onions grow, farmers are increasing the window of time in which they grow them. There are always enough suppliers and not enough takers. And that doesn't change unless there's a weather related drop in production."

It's a sad truth about farming and produce pricing, says Sobiech, "somewhere, someone must be hurt for others to profit."

At Green Valley Onion Co, the large, modern sorting and packing plant that he built in the Black Dirt, Sobiech buys hundreds of thousands of pounds of onions from Black Dirt and other growers across the U.S. every season. His plant machinery and a team of about 30 workers size and sort the onions for supermarkets. Then he repacks the various types, colors and sizes of onions into mesh bags, boxes, or crates – whatever the buyer requires.

Sobiech could sell the smaller and imperfect onions for a lower price but instead he ships them – hundreds of thousands of pounds of them over the past few years – to institutions that feed the hungry, City Harvest and the Food Bank of the Hudson Valley. Sobiech, who took over the packing business from his father, comes from a family once well known in the muck lands as onion growers.

The supermarkets that he supplies pay him as little as they can get away with, explains Sobiech. And like other re-packers, he says, "I buy the best product I can find at the best price I can get."

In recent years supermarkets paid as little as $8 and rarely as much as $12 for a 50-pound bag of the pungent, yellow onions from the Black Dirt valley. The packers break the 50-pounder down into smaller bags and sell them for what amounts to the equivalent of $50 or more for a 50-pound bag. There is a bigger profit on the hardy onion, with its longer shelf life, than on almost any other produce, especially the highly perishable and fragile crops like berries and salad greens.

But after years of slim pickings, 2014 turned out to be a bonanza year in which good weather in the Northeast pushed prices up. The Black Dirt's weary onion growers were fetching as much as $15 for a 50-pound bag in a harvest that was for many farmers the biggest in a decade or more. But as harvesting progressed it turned out to be a bumper year for farmers across the country, supplies soared and prices dropped. Some Black Dirt farmers whose crops matured late had to worry they would have to dump unsold onions.

The 2015 weather disasters that killed crops in Texas and the Pacific Northwest may have ended up providing a bonanza for Black Dirt onion farmers who again anticipated $15 for a 50-pound bag of their onions. One farmer's disaster is another's good fortune.

Some farmers grumble about the prices that local packers pay them. Farmers growing onions and a range of other produce, have increasingly become their own packers and distributors in recent years – there are about a dozen onion packers in the Black Dirt today. Sobiech, one of the biggest, says that when the onion growers become packers or distributors themselves their pricing strategy is exactly the same as the dealers they once complained about.

Not all local packers handle onions. Many are now dealing with a range of produce. Take fourth generation Black Dirt farmer Alex Kocot, a feisty, entrepreneurial 52-year-old onion farmer who started growing trendy "spring mix" baby lettuce in 2003. After some difficult years he took a huge gamble in 2012 and bought a warehouse in Newburg, near Stewart Airport, where he now packages his and other local farmer's "spring mix" crops, including that grown by muck land farmer Rick Minkus of Minkus Family Farm, a major spring mix grower, for distribution to markets all the way from Boston to Washington D.C

A small number of produce farmers avoid the distributors/packers and truck their produce directly to the vast Hunts Point Market in the Bronx. The largest wholesale produce market in the world, it covers a million square feet. Fruit and vegetables from across the United States and 55 countries are shipped in by boat, rail and tractor-trailer every day. Selling at the teeming and frenzied hub has complications: growers must provide trucks, drivers and crew to sell on consignment, pay commission to vendors and then, if produce doesn't move, pay fees for produce that has to be dumped. It's a tough route, but those few growers who have mastered the Hunts Point Market system swear that it pays.

Among them are the three Morgiewicz brothers of Morgiewicz Produce, Joe, Dan and David, who sell half their 35 varieties of produce at 10 farmers markets, and the other half wholesale at Hunts Point. Since diversification from onion crops started more than 35 years ago, growers have also been diversifying their marketing methods. "Distribution is one of the hardest issues for farmers who have never dealt with it themselves," says Cheryl Rogowski, of W. Rogowski Farms, who tried a wide range of marketing techniques since switching from onions when she took the farm over when her father died. She recalls an enthusiastic new farmer who arrived in the region and grew a bounty of crops without any plans for selling them. "At harvest time all he could do was put up a roadside stand, but it was totally inadequate."

Wholesale to Institutions

In full agreement is Frank Dagele, managing partner of Dagele Brothers Produce, the 550 acre farm which stretches across a large tract of Black Dirt between Pine Island and Florida. "Before you put the seed in the ground you have to know where it's going to be marketed. The other half of marketing is knowing that you have a customer who will pay you top dollar for top quality. After all, we are in the most populous region of the country. We should be able to find a secure, steady market for our produce." That market for the Dagele Brothers is wholesale to large institutions increasingly interested in fresh and local produce, both in New York City and Orange County.

The farm, operated by Frank, Robert and Randal Dagele, was started in 1919, when the brothers' grandparent's, John and Josephine, emigrated from Poland and settled on 40 acres. Today Dagele Bros. Produce grows cilantro, cauliflower, broccoli, Brussels sprouts, cabbage, sweet potatoes, radish, Yukon gold potatoes, fingerling potatoes, scallions, onions, leeks, garlic, celery, pumpkin, spaghetti squash, kabocha squash, delicata squash, butternut squash, acorn squash, spinach, escarole, endive, head lettuce, leaf lettuce, collards ….a range simplified as "artichokes to zucchini".

The Dagele brothers recently started providing fresh and frozen produce and fruits to the Orange County Office for the Aging which provides 900 seniors a meal a day. They are replacing a company in Houston, Texas, which used to supply the Office for the Aging by shipping their produce across the country. Contracts to supply the county jail and Meals on Wheels are in the offing, consistent with a concerted effort in the state and county for institutions to get their produce from local growers. For years Dagele Bros. has supplied the produce for schools in Goshen, Warwick, Chester and Greenwood Lake, all local areas in Orange County. "We supply everything they need," he says. "As aggregators, if we don't grow what's required, we look first to other local farms, and then go elsewhere across the U.S.."

Dagele says that schools are his niche, and he would very much like to see more school cafeterias with salad bars. But in spite of social pressure to get more healthy food in schools, he hasn't seen much of an increased demand. "I have delivered 20 boxes of romaine lettuce and a dozen boxes of bananas while right next to me is a truck delivering 1,000 boxes of fried chicken nuggets," he says. "Are schools taking advantage of the local availability of fresh produce? Absolutely not! But some are trying harder than others."

Some of the Dageles' produce is also sold retail to supermarkets and farmers markets throughout the region. Getting produce to market now often requires that farmers must do something that was never associated with farming – engaging personally with the people who buy their crops. Taking vegetables and fruit directly to the people who eat them has increasingly become the path to profits.

The Greenmarket Revolution

In 1976 when New Yorkers Barry Benepe and Bob Lewis, both qualified town planners, started the first Greenmarket in New York City, the farmers in the region were invisible, and many were going bankrupt. "Farmers were never even identified with produce," recalls Lewis, a man whose name has become synonymous with those ubiquitous open air markets that now supply fresh local fruit and vegetable to urban consumers throughout the United States.

"Farmers were commodified and they were not in a position to change that. It didn't help that at Cornell (University) and other agricultural colleges, the bias was towards large-scale production. Due to the leadership, and analytic capabilities at the time, there was a worship of scale, with scant ability to foresee changes in trends. Even the USDA was on that track. There was great pride in the massive American producers – and no attention to the taste of the produce or the viability of the farms."

Lewis recalls that farmers in Orange County, like farmers elsewhere in the greater New York region, were not organized or trained to anticipate cultural trends, such as the slow, but growing consumer demand for healthy and better tasting food. It was simple: consumers would buy, unidentified farmers would supply.

"When we started the Greenmarket consumers had never heard of the Black Dirt. Fewer than 1% had any connection with any of the region's farmers. The concept of 'local' being desirable didn't exist," recalls Lewis. "It didn't help that a lot of 'old school' farmers had the deeply ingrained view that you weren't a real farmer if you didn't sell wholesale. Going to market with your produce – it was beyond their ken."

The collaboration that led to the Greenmarket revolution started in 1975 when Lewis got a job with Benepe, an architect as well as a regional planner, at the New York State Department of Environmental and Regional Planning. Benepe was many years his senior but in outlook they were soul mates.

"We were advocates for human scale planning. The American arc had moved so far from human scale that the urban setting had become bleak. Recreating the urban markets – modern versions of the ancient Greek *agora* – wasn't about farmers and consumers alone. It was also about reviving civic institutions."

Speaking of Benepe, now 86, Lewis says: "The Greenmarkets could have happened without me, but not without him." After encountering regional farmers barely able to make a living, Benepe decided to create a retail market that could connect struggling farmers with city consumers. The concept was so mutually successful that farmers' markets sprang up across the region. Selling to the Greenmarkets became viable while fresh, local food became extremely desirable. Both Benepe and Lewis have received a number of awards that recognize their contribution to New York City life, commerce and cuisine.

"With the Greenmarkets we created the local food movement. It took 30 years for the farmer-city linkages we started in the 1970s to percolate into the system, creating that culinary and economic bond between rural farmers and urban consumers." Then in the spring of 2007 *Time Magazine* had a cover story that said it all: "Forget Organic, Go Local."

Consciousness-raising about the advantages of local food was boosted by a band of savvy chefs and food writers, who had started to exult in an indigenous cuisine. The idea that "imported must be better," that had prevailed throughout America's culinary history, was dying – or, at least, where it mattered to those who supplied local ingredients. New York City restaurants like Danny Meyers "Union Square Café" and his "Gramercy Tavern" became renowned for their emphasis on local, seasonal produce in proud American dishes. The word was spread further by Leslie Brenner's book *American Appetite* (William Morrow, 1999), a chronology of the evolution of a national American cuisine, and Danny Meyers' *Setting the Table* (Harper, 2006).

Meyers' Gramercy Tavern has long been one of the most cherished restaurants in the hearts of "foodie" New Yorkers. The chef, Michael Anthony, came from Blue Hill at Stone Barn, the apogee of "field to table" restaurants in the Northeast. It was at the Gramercy Tavern that Bob Lewis talked about the future of the Black Dirt farms that supply Greenmarkets throughout the tristate region. In the 35 years since trucks filled with fresh-picked vegetables started their pre-dawn motorcade from the muck lands to the Greenmarkets, Lewis has come to know many of the Black Dirt farmers.

Those growers who followed the route to Greenmarkets have eliminated a few middleman costs and are free to charge more or less than supermarkets and chain stores. To an extent they can set their own prices for a public that is often quite affluent, and prepared to pay a little more for fresh, locally grown produce. Now, at least 20 Black Dirt farmers are making friends with customers, developing loyalty and maybe even having a good time at farmers' markets throughout the region. Some of them supply as many as 10 farmers markets each week.

Jenny Jones, the Gramercy Tavern manager in charge of buying for the restaurant, said that "fresh and local" was so important in the kitchen that the chefs bought produce from Greenmarkets four days a week. "We go early – and we're often in line with chefs from other restaurants."

One of their favorite growers is Alex Paffenroth, the Black Dirt farmer known in the New York City restaurant world as the "root king." "He has the most wonderful sunchokes (Jerusalem artichokes). We have even asked him to grow extra for us. We often ask farmers to plant something specially for our menu," Jones said. The relationship with the growers is so important to Michael Anthony and Danny Meyers that a couple of times a year they take half a dozen restaurant staff to spend time on one of the supplying farms. "That's how things have changed in 35 years," comments Lewis. "In the restaurant world now, farmers are recognized and respected."

Community Supported Agriculture

Another symbiotic marketing system that has caught on in the Black Dirt region and beyond is Community Supported Agriculture (CSA), which creates a direct partnership between a farm and members of the community. Members pay farmers at the beginning of the season, providing them with the money they will use to pay for seeds and equipment. In return, each week they receive a share of the harvest, whatever is mature at the time.

Members commit to sharing both the benefits and risks of each season. This system gives farmers more protection from both the vagaries of nature and price fluctuations. Eliminating the people in the middle of farmer-consumer dealings gives the public a better sense of where their food comes from and a lower price for local food.

Started in Japan, CSAs were introduced in the U.S. in the 1980s and are now a distribution system on about 13,000 farms. In some rural areas, members pick up their share at the farm, while in cities, farmers drop off produce at distribution sites. Some CSA adaptations now allow senior or poorer members to pay weekly and some, like J.A.D.S. farm market in Pine Island, let members select which parts of the harvest they want. Some urban CSA systems even deliver to the workplace.

At the Union Square Greenmarket one fall morning Andy Kurosz, a Black Dirt honey producer, took a brief break from the busy Rogowski Farms stand where he was selling fresh produce, to deliver the farms' CSA weekly harvest to Wen-Jay Ying of Brooklyn. In her van parked off the square, Ying collects harvests destined for Brooklyn CSA members. After reading an article on the decrease of supermarkets in New York City and an increased dependency on purchasing fresh produce at bodegas, Ying founded Local Roots NYC which provides more than 350 NYC residents with local, sustainably grown food.

Ying, who won The Entrepreneur Award from New York Mayor Michael Bloomberg in 2013 for her work promoting CSAs in the region, says the distribution system has now expanded to producers of other products, including cheese, baked goods, meat, fish and herbs. And a growing number of Black Dirt farmers are offering CSA shares to members in Orange County as well as in the wider tristate area.

Farm Bill and the Black Dirt

There was a lot of attention paid to the massive cuts in food stamps in the 2013 Farm Bill, signed into law by President Barack Obama early in 2014. Many produce farmers are involved in the various state and federally funded programs that help pay for food for the poor. Cuts in these programs not only hurt poorer consumers trying to buy healthy, fresh produce, they hurt farmers everywhere, including the Black Dirt region. Farmers supplying poorer areas might get 90% of their payments from funded coupons.

Chris Pawelski, the farmer who lobbies for specialty crop farmers, is pushing a block grant program that would partner specialty crop producers with food banks, food recovery programs and food pantries and bye-pass repackers and terminal markets.

He writes on his new blog www.farmroot.org: "This program would deliver fresh quality produce directly from the farmer to organizations that serve the food insecure. It would be administered by states to qualifying food banks, food recovery programs and food pantries. Grant recipients would be required to purchase fresh produce directly from farmers rather than via re-packers or at terminal markets. This new proposed program (which is already being done by some food recovery organizations through private donations) would further strengthen the ties between the agricultural and nutrition titles of the Farm Bill."

Tax-payer contributions to farmers in the United States have become controversial – especially the multi-million-dollar payouts to vast monoculture farms growing corn, soybeans, wheat, cotton and rice, mostly in the Midwest. Environmentalists have taken issue with tax-payer money supporting agriculture that they believe is harming the environment. The Environmental Working Group (EWG), a non-profit concerned with toxic chemicals and health issues, used the Freedom of Information Act to obtain the full amount of government funds to farmers by state, county and farm, 1995-2012, and made all the information available online.

Some local conservationists have taken up the issue of "subsidies" listed by the EWG being paid to Black Dirt farmers because most use conventional farming practices, including pesticides. They see it as taxpayers' money being used to subsidize polluters. (A few muck land farmers take no federal funds at all.) A spokesman at the United States Department of Agriculture Farm Service Agency (FSA) in Middletown, NY, said that in the case of local specialty crop farmers, using the term "subsidies" was misleading.

Most funding for Black Dirt Farmers was related to crop insurance – the cost of policies for farmers and then the payment to farmers for damaged or destroyed crops. Part of the policy is paid by the farmer and those farmers who don't take out insurance get no payments for crop losses.

Crop insurance was recently improved by the Farm Bill of 2014, and, of benefit to many Black Dirt farms, it now covers diversified crops. But it also costs farmers more. To be eligible for crop-loss payments, farmers must keep regular, time consuming, detailed records.

Another federal payment to the U.S. farming economy, including the muck lands growers, is the United States Department of Agriculture project called CREP, for Conservation Reserve Enhancement Program. It has been paying landowners between $350 and $495 an acre a year to put down grass cover and leave the land fallow. The largest private land conservation program in the United States, it is managed by the Farm Service Agency and participation is voluntary.

This well-intentioned program was a measure to prevent erosion of land bordering the rivers and creeks. But under an exception for the Black Dirt valley, the whole region became eligible for CREP. Since CREP payments are higher than the rent farmers can get for their land, those with land they did not want to farm often signed up for CREP payments rather than rent their fields to farming neighbors. CREP land-owners are required to follow maintenance rules, including weed control and mowing but some are delinquent. Farm neighbors complain that overgrown fallow lands are home to flamboyant bugs, invasive nuisance weeds and hungry wildlife which eat their seedlings in the spring.

The program, which was even criticized by some farmers who collecting CREP payments, has now been replaced by other conservation measures. But CREP signatories must see their 10 to 15 year contracts through their terms or pay fines.

One other program giving federal aid to farmers is the USDA's Natural Resources Conservation Service, which helps those who follow specified conservation methods to pay the cost of laying down cover crops and clearing drainage ditches – all especially important in the conditions that prevail in the muck lands.

"There are no free handouts in the program. Farmers have to go through a million hoops. Money won't be given out if farms don't follow certain conservation practices, and if later they are not compliant, the money must be given back," said the FSA spokesman who added the view that the farmers of the valley were environmentally conscientious. "They love the land, and they love the job the do. They are certainly not in it for the money."

Even if they were in it just for profits, the prospects for farming would become bleak if farmers didn't take appropriate care of their land. No one is more realistic about that than farmers themselves. But with continual threats of flooding and no remedy in sight for the farm labor shortages, no matter how sustainably the farmers husband their land, the big question arises: What is the Black Dirt region's future? ■

CHAPTER 10: THE FARMLAND'S FUTURE

"...we need not only to celebrate farmers, but also to advocate for them."

The Black Dirt region's bucolic beauty, its proximity to the demographically expanding tristate region and rising regional land values could possibly, in years to come, create pressures to remove restrictions that prevent building or development on the muck lands. Perhaps new construction technologies – no matter how expensive – could make building in this farmland both possible and viable. Maybe the determined wealthy could dig out the chernozem and replace it with buildable, drainable soil.

Perhaps some anxious environmentalists consider all these scenarios to be possible. But their concern would not be over the loss of productive farmland to development. Rather, their dismay would be over the loss of potential wetlands for wildlife and birds. For a group of conservationists the preferred plan is to let the Wallkill River flood the valley, allow the Black Dirt farms to revert to a swamp, and do it now, making it unappealing and possibly irremediable for future development, or agriculture. Allowing the

Wallkill Valley to return to a permanent swamp is consistent with their view that wherever possible, the environment should revert to its original or natural state. It's an argument that would not amuse the billions of people fed by farmers growing crops in the vast drained floodplains of the world – The Mississippi Delta, The Nile Valley, The Tigris-Euphrates Delta....

However, the idea of letting parts of the valley revert to wetland as a way of actually preventing flooding of farmlands has been proposed by Michael Edelstein, co-president of the non-profit Orange Environment, Inc. A professor of Environmental Psychology at Ramapo College, NJ, he wrote after the devastating flooding in the Black Dirt valley caused by Hurricane Irene:

> I propose that Orange Environment, working with all
> stakeholders and agencies, develop a plan for conversion
> of strategic Black Dirt areas to wetlands, using federal
> funds. As part of the plan, an agreement would be
> reached with the government to support continued
> farming on the bulk of the black dirt with the hope
> that flooding there would be controlled in the process.

He says no authority, government or otherwise, has so far followed up on his suggestion.

With Orange Environment, for more than 25 years Edelstein has been fighting the county, mainly in court, over issues related to pollution of the Wallkill River from the landfill, which was illegally built on wetlands. He believes that removal of wetlands that absorbed much of the floodwaters has been a major contributor to the extreme flooding in recent years.

Any consideration of the future of the Black Dirt valley has to look at the rapid rate at which New York is losing farmland. Almost 450,000 acres of New York agricultural acreage – about 4,500 medium sized farms – has been turned into commercial or residential property since 1982. Many of the farms still functioning in the Hudson Valley, especially dairy farms, are struggling to stay profitable in the face of lower priced competition from out-of-state, overseas competitors and market prices that don't rise while costs do.

That unstoppable gobbling up of farms for development makes the highly productive Black Dirt farmland more important, strategically and economically. Not only are local authorities who govern the region recognizing that the muck lands are a vital resource, so soon will many of the millions of people in the greater tristate area whose supply of fresh healthy vegetables will increasingly be supplied by Black Dirt growers, fresher and at lower cost than those transported across the U.S. – as long as they can continue to farm. The demand for this locally grown produce should swell, and with it, one hopes, the public willingness to fight for Black Dirt farmers and for whatever measures must be taken to keep their fertile valley drained, supplied with legal labor, and economically viable.

Famed food writer and blogger/columnist Mark Bittman wrote in the *New York Times* a tribute to the pleasures of fresh, locally grown produce. "But to get these beautiful veggies," he wrote, "we need real farmers who grow real food, and the will to reform a broke food system. And for that, we need not only celebrate farmers, but also to advocate for them."

Even those environmentalists who would prefer that the muck lands become swamplands must heed the powerful argument on the carbon emissions that are avoided if produce is acquired from just 60 miles away, rather than trucked across the country. Maire Ullrich did the math and estimates that about 36,960,000 pounds of carbon are NOT released into the atmosphere annually if produce is acquired from the Black Dirt valley, instead of transported from farms in the western states.

But preserving the great basin of Black Dirt for farming is superfluous (so to speak) if there aren't farmers. Alex Kocot, 52, who mainly grows onions and salad greens, is among those who worry that "the next generation doesn't have what it takes. They have too many distractions. Here, you have to focus 10, 12, 14 hours a day. It's a total sacrifice during growing season because crops don't wait. Timing is 80% of success. Kids have to know how to work. It's hard, it's hard," says Kocot.

It is certain that if conditions become untenable – for example, the river continues to flood, there is insufficient labor to plant and harvest, and low prices make farming unprofitable – farmers will pack up and leave, as many did in the late 1980s. At that time the market was overwhelmed with cheap imports from the West coast, the high dollar increased imports from Canada, consumers began to favor sweet onions and the public started to eat out more which grew the markets for large, institutional and fast-food friendly onions rather than the small pungent onion grown in the region. For many it was just too difficult to make a living as an onions-only farmer.

For most Black Dirt growers, including those growing onions, 2014 was a fabulous year – the first bountiful year in many. And 2015 wound up as another winner for farmers in the region. A couple more years of severe weather events and catastrophic flooding would not just make the land non-arable it would wipe out growers' financial reserves and their emotional resolve. After Hurricane Irene in 2011 many farmers' losses were almost overwhelming. But just as they had after weather disasters in the past, the farmers knuckled down, refinanced and started again.

But There's a Limit!

The sign that people are losing hope is called Impermanence Syndrome, a condition recognized by economists and industrial psychologists. It occurs when businesses and individuals believe their future is both poor, and out of their control. As a result, they do not make the necessary investments in their businesses and no longer use best management practices. Of course, the attitude becomes self-fulfilling.

Impermanence Syndrome has been common in agricultural areas threatened by suburban expansion. It also occurs when the viability of the business is so threatened that others in the industry – fellow farmers – begin to close up shop. A study on the future of farming in Orange County, done by researchers at the University of Nebraska at Lincoln in 2008, found little sign of Impermanence Syndrome here. Almost 70% of those under 55 expected to be farming in ten years. Among factors that influenced their optimism was whether they had children or grandchildren who would succeed them as operators, and the expectation of a strong future market for their produce: Future Farmers and Growing Markets.

The Future Farmers

"Don't let your children grow up to be farmers." It was the headline on an op-ed article by Bren Smith in the *New York Times* (Aug 9, 2014) He points out that 91% of farmers must rely on other sources of income. In the 1880s, 1930s and 1970s farmer organizations were protesting and lobbying. "We need to take the lead in shaping a new food economy …" he writes. For future farmers he advocates for "a new food economy that ensures good food also means making a good living."

"Mothers and fathers won't be encouraged to train their kids to farm if they have no faith in the future," says Maire Ullrich of the CCE. "But I don't see that happening." She estimates that at least half the farms in the region will be handed down or bought by descendents raised on the farms. "There was a time in the 70s and 80s when farm families didn't encourage their kids to be farmers. There are not so many farmers aged between 30 and 45. But the culture changed. Now many young people want to work in the soil."

The State of Agriculture in the Hudson Valley, the 2007 study by Glynwood, an agricultural non-profit in Cold Spring, NY, concluded that farmers were aging out. The average age was 57 then and experienced farmers were nearing retirement. But there was an increase in the age of farmers under 25.

Among the younger sons of the black soil is Brennan Sobiech, sixth generation progeny of a family long associated with onion farming. "He was smart and had good grades. But he never wanted to do anything other than be a farmer," says Brennan's father, Ed Sobiech, an onion packer. Brennan was just 15 when his father started to teach him how to be a serious onion grower. At 17 Brennan started farming onions solo on 70-acres in the Western edge of the Mission Land.

In the fall, when Brennan's onions were all harvested, he was putting his farm equipment away. "What I like is the field work, being outside on the tractor. And right now there's good money in onions, especially if I grow early, and then harvest before the price drops at the end of the season."

Long term, he wants to farm about 100 acres, with 30 in soybeans. "Normally you get 35-40 bushels an acre, but here in the muck you get 65-75 bushels. And it's a great rotation crop with onions. You plow it right back into the soil."

Describing a routine that most 20-year-olds would find exceedingly rigorous, he said: "I begin in the fields early March. I start plowing when its still dark, say 4.30 am, and go on until 9.30 at night. No weekends off!"

Through the season he sprays for weeds, bugs and disease, using some pesticides exceedingly sparingly because they cost a fortune. To kill the deadly enemy of the onion, the miniscule thrips bug, he must spray at night. "So I start at about 10.30 pm and go right through until I'm finished at about 8.30 in the morning."

Because he uses Integrated Crop Management practices his fall fields were covered with barley, a cover crop that prevents soil from being lost to the wind or washed away. In the spring he plows the barley into the soil. "For me, I find farming very satisfying if you have a good year, like it was my first year on my own, 2012. But sometimes it really gets you down. The next year there were 15 inches of rain in June. It was tough – specially getting (my tractor) stuck in the muck. I really don't see a lot of kids around here going into farming. They see how tough it can be."

But there is one advantage for this next generation of Black Dirt farmers: they all get along. "It's not like it was for the older generations when there was so much bad blood." He mentions his good friends, Joe and Tom Minkus, who work with their father Rick Minkus on the Minkus Family Farm in the western region of the Black Dirt valley. The Minkus brothers will take over what is the largest onion producing farm in the county and the largest produce farming operation in the Black Dirt, with over 1,000 acres of owned and leased land.

Rick Minkus is that rare person in the Black Dirt, a large scale farmer with no ancestry in the region. He bought a share in a 60 acre farm in 1993 and after buying out his partner some years ago has expanded the operation into a diversified business, both packing and growing a large range of produce for sale wholesale to retailers throughout the tristate region.

After days of record winter snowfall in 2014, when the Minkus farm stretched like the tundra into the distant tree line, Tom Minkus, 27, was fixing machinery. He worked in a large, cold barn, doing repairs to a lettuce seed planter, calibrating the two electric motors that each drops seed in a straight row for "spring mix", the tender green leaf combination that is much loved by foodies.

He explained that when he was in the 11th and 12th grades at high school he was also attending the local BOCES (Board of Cooperative Educational Services) Vocational Technical for High School students to learn heavy equipment mechanics, skills that are highly valued on a big diversified produce farm. "I was never really interested in school," he smiles. "I always wanted to be on the move."

Apart from 300 acres of onions, Minkus Family Farms also grows 500 acres of soybeans, 150 acres of field corn and 300 acres of spring mix, which gives three harvests each summer. "Like my brother Joe, I do whatever needs to be done on the farm." The two were working on creating a spraying device with a 90 foot span – a mechanical feat.

"I like being my own boss, even though the hours are long and we start early, like 4:30 am. When others are out having fun in the summer, we are out in the fields – the Black Dirt Beach."

The Minkus farm is bordered by the Wallkill River and is affected by all the same travails as others in the region, including labor shortages and vulnerability to flooding. After Hurricane Irene some of the barns were two feet deep in water. Still, in spite of the recent history of flooding Tom Minkus is optimistic about the future and believes others his age are too. "Those people in farming now – they will all stay on the farms. And as long as there is Black Dirt available, people are going to farm it."

Greg DeBuck, 32, son of Leonard of DeBuck's Sod Farm, never had any doubt about following in his father's footsteps. He went to Pennsylvania State University where he studied Turfgrass Science, a four-year degree, and then came home to help run the 300-acre farm, taking over much of the operations from his father, as well as Scenic Valley Golf Course, an off-shoot of the sod farm. It was Greg who was operating the giant sod harvester at dawn one day late in the summer, when mist rising off the moist muck plain created the hazy pink skyline for which the valley is renowned.

Greg was enjoying driving the machine, a massive futuristic-looking multi-tasker that slowly sliced, rolled and stacked the strips of turf. As he drove across the misty turf it became clear there was a little boy by his side in the cab. Four year old John DeBuck was already learning how to harvest, as children did 100 years ago. Asked what he wanted to be when he grew up, little John said "A Rock Star!" A future farmer for sure.

An earnest, good natured young man who already plays a leadership role in the community, Greg is a Black Dirt farming devotee. "There are three factors that work well for us here: our proximity to the huge tristate market, our neighbors are all farmers so we can help each other, and third, no one complains about engine noise in the early hours! But it is a hard life," he adds, "too hard if your heart isn't in it."

But once your heart is in it, it's hard to let go, even for those who went to college to study for other professions like Michelle Gurda, 24. Tall, strong and sweet-natured, Michelle was a star on the college tennis team at Adelphi University, Long Island, where she graduated with a degree in marketing and human resources in 2013. Bypassing the lucrative hubbub of New York, she came straight home to A. Gurda Farms, where she and her younger sister Taylor had grown up. She started helping her father, Andrew Gurda, on a parcel on the Mission Land.

Andrew Gurda operates a packing business, working in collaboration with his brothers Dave and Jerry Gurda, who grow a wide variety of produce as Davandjer Farms (derived from Dave, Andrew and Jerry) on an adjacent 200-acre stretch of muck land. Dave and Jerry do the growing, while Andrew mostly does packing and distributing. He also deals with organic produce shipped in from elsewhere, since the Black Dirt is so inhospitable to organic farming methods.

Michelle was using her skills in the office, doing the books and ensuring that the operations at the Gurda warehouses were in compliance with Safe Quality Foods (SQF) standards, a certification that is required by some of the stores they supply.

After working at the family farm for a year after graduating, Michelle decided to take a break from farming and join a division of the county government called Orange County Partnership. "I've been around farming since a baby. I was on a tractor when I was seven. As a woman going into farming I think it's a great business and I love it. But I need to explore what's out there for a while. My Dad encourages me. He says the farm will still be here when I'm ready to return."

Michelle is confident about the future. "I believe that on most of the farms there's a young person in the family who wants to take it over. My generation are driven to succeed and with new technology it will be even better than ever to be a farmer. New technology will require less manpower than before. What took four people will take just one. Even doing the books will be more efficient. And people will collaborate, help each other," says Michelle, who is a friend of Tom Minkus and Brennan Sobiech.

"We look at things differently now," agreed Kelsey Lain, 27, who graduated from Quinnipiac University, CT, with a degree in communications, and came straight home to work on her parents' 1,000-acre sod and soybean farm, most of it flanking the volatile Wallkill River. Now that marketing and public relations has become a component of modern farming, Kelsey said her degree gave her the confidence and skills to be very useful in the farm office.

She recently married Brandon Gurda, 28, a fifth generation son of the Gurda family (Michelle's father Andy is his uncle), whose love for the soil inspired him to start his own landscaping business when he was still in high school. While Brandon manages his Gurda Landscaping, now a booming business, and occasionally helps Chip Lain on the sod and soybean farm, Kelsey manages the office at Pineturf Nursery. One day, when Chip and Shari retire, the two will run the Lain farm.

One of the problems Kelsey was dealing with was looking for workers, young people who could learn to do all the varied jobs required in their operations, including handling the technically sophisticated equipment. Because, as labor shortages persist, increasingly farm owners are turning to machinery that eliminates human manual labor. And that equipment requires a different worker than those who have traditionally worked the fields – a worker with mechanical and literary skills. Yet recruiting people adept at driving complicated agricultural machinery was only part of her management problem. "Some people can't handle the hours. You tell them we start at 3:30 in the morning, but they don't believe you. In this business if they arrive late you have to fire them."

Its not that Kelsey doesn't put her own hands in the soil. While managing the office, she started planting tomatoes and corn in a few acres of Black Dirt beside the sod fields. Her harvest was sold at a table beside the office with such success she is expanding her garden. But Brandon and Kelsey's first child, a sixth generation Gurda, was born in the spring of 2014, slowing some of Kelsey's farming ambitions.

What happens when none of the offspring want to take over the farm? What does the retiring farmer do? Aging farmers here can't, like farmers elsewhere, sell their land to a developer for retirement income and head to Florida for a quiet, financially secure life in the sun. Typically, retiring muck land farmers approach their neighboring growers and ask if they are interested in acquiring more land. As the economics of modern farming often require larger tracts, these land deals are frequently done between farmers without ever involving professional realtors. Established farmers predict that the way of the future is that large farms will simply get larger.

But sometimes the future farmers taking over available land in Black Dirt valley are those romantic first-time farmers, people who are leaving the white-collar world to fulfill a lifetime's yearning. Typical is Tony Bracco, a graphic artist with a business in New Jersey, who, in his fifties, bought 25 acres off County Route 1.

"That was in 2009 and I had a great first harvest the following year. But in 2011 Hurricane Irene came and we lost everything." With another business to provide some income for the family, Bracco was able to gradually start again, rebuild his greenhouse and fill his fields with produce.

"We have never put a chemical on the place," says Bracco proudly. The large sign he erected at the roadside reads "Non-GMO. Sustainable." In his new greenhouse he showed off young kale, collard greens and spinach. Out in his fields there were remnants of the summer harvest – zucchini, egg-plant, heirloom tomatoes and peppers. He supplies high-end country clubs in New Jersey and many farm-to-table and fine dining restaurants in both New York and New Jersey.

Tony Bracco was at his farm one fall Sunday making repairs. With him on the farm that chilly day was his 10-year-old son Anthony Jr., who is as passionate about farming as his Dad, and accompanies him to the plot sev-eral times a week - at every opportunity that his school work allows. "In-stead of weedkiller," explained the child farmer, "we use a thin plastic groundcover which we spread with special machines. It cuts the weeding time to one tenth."

In the summer of 2014 Tony and Christa Bracco, his wife and farm partner, put up a canopy on their uplands beside County Route 1, and started a weekend farm stand. In spite of the tiresome weeding that their chemical-free farming approach requires, the family's enthusiasm about their new farm is abundant. Their plans for the future include providing CSAs, growing micro greens in the greenhouse, and one day maybe fruit trees. Customers are allowed to step out into the fields and stroll through the rows of growing produce. In the spring of 2015, the family put out picnic ta-bles and a smart new stand. "I want it to be a place people can just come, sit and enjoy themselves," says Tony.

Also typical of those who left successful professions in the white col-lar world for the agricultural lifestyle are Will Brown and Barbara Felton of Lowland Farm alongside the Pochuck Creek. Brown, an economist, and Fel-ton, a psychologist, lived and worked in New York City for 30 years before they moved to the Warwick Valley.

They purchased the bucolic stretch of pastures and woodlands adja-cent to the Black Dirt valley in 1985 as a weekend and summer home, al-lowing neighbors to graze cattle on the land. But they were inspired to become farmers themselves, and in 2004 they bought their own cows. In synch with the sensibilities around them, they dedicated themselves to rais-ing purely grass fed beef. None of the animals are given antibiotics and grow naturally, free of growth-promoting hormones.

Before long Brown and Felton were also raising pork, lamb, and chick-ens using the same sustainable methods, and have now added bees and honey to their farm repertoire – the white collar world a distant memory.

The idea of growing crops for a fine brew inspired Rich Coleman and his late wife Amanda, to leave their white-collar life. The couple moved to the Westtown region from New Jersey three years ago to grow hops, a crop new to the region, though New York State was the nation's largest hops producer before diseases wiped it off the agricultural landscape more than 50 years ago.

While running a food service business from his home in Westtown, on the edge of the muck lands, Coleman has planted several acres of hops, expanding his acreage every year, and is collaborating with Black Dirt farm neighbors who are growing barley for Coleman's brews.

State legislation allowing on-farm tastings of beer and liquor passed in 2014. So, Coleman joined a growing beverage industry in the Black Dirt region, which includes the new Orange County Distillery situated on a Black Dirt farm near Goshen, and the Warwick Valley Winery and Distillery, situated off Little York Road. In the fall of 2014 he set up tables on his property where customers could "sit out in the sun, enjoy the view of the hops and taste the beer." His brew house on the hill has become a huge hit, drawing crowds every weekend.

New Farmers

A wide, generous network of programs at county, state and federal level exists to help new farmers get access to loans and land they cannot afford, and the training they need. The Farm Bill signed in January 2014 included provisions to help younger Americans and veterans who are entering the agricultural sector. (The average cost of Black Dirt at the start of 2015 was $6,000 an acre for flood-safe farmland and about $2,500 close to the flood zones.)

For over 100 years the Northeast Beginning Farmers Project, housed at the Cornell University Small Farmers Program, Ithaca, NY, has been helping new farmers and ranchers, whether they are getting started, diversifying or running into trouble. The project, which had USDA funding of $19 million in 2014, provides courses, videos, training and mentoring.

The Agrarian Trust is a newly founded private, nationwide organization helping to make land accessible to new farmers and enable them to get the skills they need. And there are many more institutions available as incubators for future farmers throughout the region.

A new project to help join farmers and investors has been started right here in the Black Dirt by the Northeast Farm Access, LLC, based in New Hampshire. Its goal is "to revive and transform sustainable agriculture --

yielding not just abundant clean, local food, but also a new generation of successful organic farmers." With support from investors they buy land, and lease it affordably to intermediate-level farmers.

They helped create the Chester Agricultural Center, LLC, the group which plans to lease up to 270 acres in the Black Dirt near Chester to farmers who otherwise could not afford the land. Among the investors in the Chester Agricultural Center is the Ralph E. Ogden Foundation in Mountainville, NY, whose aim is to conserve farmland and encourage organic farming.

"One of the biggest challenges facing Hudson Valley farmers, especially beginning farmers, is finding farmland," says David Haight, New York State director of the American Farmland Trust (AFT). The trust is the one national conservation organization dedicated to protecting farmland, promoting sound farming practices and keeping farmers on the land.

"Since the early 1980s, New York has lost half a million acres of farmland to real estate development. That's the equivalent of 4,500 farms," says Haight. The importance of keeping land in agriculture has become an imperative. As a result, the AFT has linked with Hudson Valley Farmlink, Orange County Land Trust, Cornell Cooperative extension and other concerned groups to help farmers – whether new or expanding – to lease that farmland whose owners don't want to, or can no longer, keep it in agriculture.

Many of the new farmers in the muck lands, predicts John Lupinski of the Orange County Farm Bureau, will be a new breed of immigrants, mainly Asian and Latino, who, like many of the Poles and German immigrants who preceded them, come from agricultural backgrounds, an ancestry associated with the soil. They will grow ethnically specific herbs and vegetables connected to their own cultural cuisines and new to the Black Dirt, on small plots, he said.

Lupinski noted that many farmers are aging out – he estimates that a third of farmers are over 65. "The key to farming in the future is that it must be seen as a business. Growers in the future have got to push a sharp pencil and not make mistakes. The future is going to be young, energetic and to a growing extent, it's going to be ethnic."

One of the projects that successfully trained new immigrants who wanted to farm was the New Farmer Development Program, started in New York City by Greenmarket with the help of Bob Lewis in 1976. "The demand for produce is growing faster than farmers can provide. So I started looking for new immigrants who already had agricultural experience, and in a year or two, could be selling at the Greenmarkets." That program grew to be FARMroots (part of GROWnyc) which is now available at a fee to all the Greenmarket farmer community of more than 230 producers, not just immigrants, and provides a wide range of technical assistance in workshops and panel discussions. About half a dozen farmers of Mexican background trained in the FARMroots program are now growing in the Black Dirt region on leased or purchased land, and selling in the Greenmarket system.

Future Markets

To entice more farmers into the Black Dirt, as much as to keep existing farm families here, the farming business has to have realistic prospects of remaining profitable and even expanding. And indications are that the market for locally grown fresh produce will see a boom, not just because the consuming population is growing but also because of growing public awareness of the connection between fresh food and health.

Even fast food companies are changing their menus to meet this new demand. Early in 2015 Shake Shack, a new fast food company that started out from a cart in Madison Square Garden, New York, and was hugely popular with Manhattan and Brooklyn foodies because it emphasized fresh and local, had a very successful Initial Public Offering on the New York Stock Exchange.

The possibility of a huge new market for onions has been opened by the new relationship that early in 2015 President Barak Obama established with Cuba. The country was once a major importer of the small onions favored by Cuban cuisine that grow beautifully in the Black Dirt soil. The bountiful onion export business was closed down when the U.S. embargoed exports to Fidel Castro's Cuba in the 1960s.

Another new market for local produce could spring to life beside the Wallkill River in Goshen, where a major producer of prepared meals made from organic or natural foods is building a 580,000 sq ft plant. Construction on Amy's Kitchen's $100 million plant is expected to start in 2016.

Amy's Kitchen is a privately-held firm with a portfolio of over 250 organic products. The company offers a range of frozen entrees, pizza, burritos, wraps, soups, beans, salsa and pasta sauce, as well as sweets, including cakes, cookies and candy bars. In the Black Dirt region exultation over Amy's Kitchen comes with reservations, however. The proportion of Black Dirt produce that is grown "Organic or Natural" is limited because of the nature of the soil. Another concern about Amy's Kitchen is that many of the 700 jobs it promises will be competing with farmers for workers. At a time when farm labor is critically short, Black Dirt growers are worried.

Since locally grown and supplied food plays a role in limiting carbon emissions from cross country transportation, contributes to healthier eating, and is important to the success of local economies, it is axiomatic that more Government bodies and elected officials are becoming engaged in promoting consumption of locally grown, nutritious food – putting money where their mouths are.

The Farm Bill, signed into law in January 2014, includes provisions that promote locally grown produce and farmers' markets. Both at the State and New York City level measures have been passed to encourage institutions to "buy local." Called "Food Metrics," their goal is to establish a serious food purchasing, tracking and reporting system that would provide decision makers with critical data on agencies' procurement practices, including how much money agencies spend on local food versus those purchased from outside New York, and whether local food was available at that time for purchase as an alternative to non-local food.

Apart from schools, hospitals and other institutions, more fresh grown local produce is required to meet the growing demand for restaurants – 24,000 of them in the New York City area alone. A supply outlet for local produce for restaurants on a much larger scale than Greenmarket provides could be the answer to the new demand. Bob Lewis who co-founded Greenmarket says plans are now going ahead to establish a facility where local produce farmers can sell wholesale to restaurants – perhaps at a specially equipped unit at the Hunts Point Market in the Bronx. As Lewis sees it, the demand will be so great that Black Dirt farmers will be motivated to put more land in production. That's why, says Lewis, "the Black Dirt region is the Market Garden for New York City."

Indeed, the market for fresh and local seem to keep growing. "Farm to Flight" operations are ensuring that fresh produce gets to in-flight catering, and Farm to Cart is the slogan for those promoting local and fresh, healthy food at street venders.

New start-ups are also helping get produce to markets. According to the *New York Times*, venture capital money is flowing into online food hubs whose purpose is to link consumers with farms. Among them is FarmersWeb, the successful and growing online marketplace formed by three Manhattanites in 2011 to connect local farmers with buyers from every kind of institution that provides food, from restaurants in Queens to private clubs in Manhattan to universities on Long Island. This kind of online marketing could well be the path of the future farmer.

Visions of a spectacular Black Dirt valley filled with abundance comes in many forms and from many quarters. Charlie Lain, now 84, still has the same futuristic dream for the valley he had when he started out with 15 acres more than 50 years ago. He envisions it all covered by a dome, a mega- greenhouse, where produce is grown year round, all powered by thermal energy.

Charlie's 15-acres is now his son Chip Lain's farm, 1,000 acres of sod, soybeans and barley beside the Wallkill River. Between them they've seen weather disasters, floods, markets collapsing and labor shortages. But none of that has changed Charlie Lain's dream of an agricultural Shangri-la under a vast dome, or his son Chip's continuing expansion of his farm in the valley, or Chip's daughter Kelsey's desire to spend her life working on the farm.

The verdict must be that for Black Dirt produce farmers the demand and markets can only grow. If there can be resolution to the two major threats to farming in the bountiful valley – the Wallkill River flooding and the growing shortage of farm workers – the future could be fantastic, both for those who want fresh produce and those who grow it. As Maire Ullrich points out, the region has many important components of a flourishing market garden: there's the fertile soil, an existing farming community with a proven ability to be productive, a strong infrastructure that supports agriculture, a range of support services and the backdrop of the tristate population, one of the wealthiest in the nation.

Existential Rewards

But none of the possibilities will come to pass if there isn't sufficient existential reward for those who make it happen – the farmers. That existential satisfaction is what keeps smart people in farming even when the weather is grim, the risks are high, the profits are low, the work is hard, regulations are endless, and there is almost constant public denigration of farmers from activist quarters. Those existential rewards come from being involved with nature, of being outdoors, of having people you know and care about working alongside you in the fields year after year, the pleasures of a home based business, the spiritual quality of seeing produce rising out of the soil, the powerful personal rewards of getting your crop to market, and, for some, seeing consumers pick up that produce, feel and smell and smile, and pay you money.

What also gives existential satisfaction to Black Dirt's specialty crop family farmers – like farmers everywhere – is that in the world of food and health, farmers are finally being given appropriate respect and recognition, and not just for the quality, range and freshness of the food they grow. They are now beginning to get appreciation for their contribution to the wellbeing of a vast and growing demographic: The biggest mouth in America.

POST SCRIPT

©Jia Han Dong

CHAPTER 11: WHAT'S UP? ISLAND LIFE

"The Black Dirt region, and Pine Island at its core, is the future,
the productive heart of the whole Warwick valley."

Black Dirt Booze

For many living in the region in the early part of the 20th Century, Pine Island was simply the hamlet at the crossroads, the place in the farmlands that you passed through on your way somewhere else. But by the 1950s Pine Island became associated with what happened in the hamlet at night.

Historian/farmer John Ruszkiewicz recalls that in those days "farmers would work all day and then head over to Rinky Dink's bar, or stop at Stanley's bar. There was the bar at the Pine Island Hotel, and the place Gus Zygmunt owned called Squabbies. There was the bar at the Polish Legion and that one all the way up Pulaski Highway at Quaker Creek...the place was filled with watering holes, and everyone had their favorite."

Between the 1950s and 1990s there were more than five bars right in the heart of the tiny hamlet, which had a population of about 1,000 at the time. More drinking establishments were scattered around the Black Dirt farming region. Youngsters from Warwick, Florida and other surrounding areas would come to Pine Island to sip their way from tavern to tavern. These sometimes rowdy joints, filled with locals winding down, were the connective tissue of the community, where neighbors hung out, caught up, got drunk, argued and made up – or maybe didn't. It was where farmers came to talk about crops, market prices and daily travails.

The farming community was the mainstay of the pubs and some old-timers in the Black Dirt argue that the disappearance of the many drinking establishments contributed to disharmony – though domestic harmony might have greatly improved.

In the late 1950s and early 60s, cars struck several people as they walked, perhaps unsteadily, home through Pine Island's unlighted streets. Local citizens banded together in 1961 to form a Chamber of Commerce to lobby for street lighting, among other community issues. (One of the motivations was to articulate the vehement opposition in the farming community to a jetport that the Port Authority of New York planned to build on the Black Dirt. The plan was eventually dropped.) Stanley Schultz, one of the founding members who lived in Pine Island until his death in 2010, once said with a chuckle that in its early years the chamber would meet at a different pub every month and it seemed they were seldom at the same pub in a year.

Gus Zygmunt, whose father played a prominent role in businesses in the hamlet in the 1950s, recalls that German settlers fraternized the Sundown bar (now his office), while those of Polish heritage went to Stanley's Bar and Rinky Dinks, further westward on County Route 1. There were frequent fights between people who didn't get on. "Most of it was jealousy," he said, shaking his head. "It was crazy."

Because of stricter enforcement of drunk driving laws and shifting social customs over the past 30 years, one by one the bars closed. Apart from the bar at the Crystal Inn, Gus Zygmunt's restaurant in Amity on the eastern outskirts of the hamlet, there was only one bar tucked inside the Polish Legion of American Veterans Post 16, close to the crossroads. The PLAV says everyone is welcome at the comfortably renovated establishment, including non-Poles and non-veterans (though some patrons say that message hasn't fully reached a few of the old-timers.)

So for a number of years, Pine Island remained a one-bar hamlet. But there's a new drinking life coming to the former Onion Capital of the World, much of it discovered at the end of quiet lanes, behind ordinary storefronts and in country barns.

On the Eastern end of the Black Dirt region, off a narrow, country road winding along Mount Eve, is the Warwick Valley Winery and Distillery, with a restaurant and home bakery and outdoor seating on a spacious lawn. This Grizzanti family business started as an apple orchard more than 25 years ago and has blossomed into one of the most successful entertainment venues in the Warwick Valley. Live music outdoors in the summer draws hundreds of people. Families from the tristate region and Pennsylvania come to spread out on the lawn and sip and munch in country style, while listening to bands play folk, blues, country or rock.

Daily tastings feature the Warwick Valley Winery wines and its award winning Doc's Hard Cider. In 2002 co-owners Jason Grizzanti and Jeremy Kidde got a license to distill fruit. The cordial distilling business expanded to include a growing repertoire of spirits. In 2013 they built a 4,000 square foot distillery with a 60-foot still tower on a small island in the Black Dirt. Here they are able to produce Warwick Rustic American Dry Gin, Black Dirt Bourbon and Black Dirt Applejack at 20 times their previous output and supply bars and restaurants throughout the region including New York City. Tastings are held at the winery at 114 Little York Road every day.

Orange County Distillery

Early in 2015, with snow deep on the black soil, fifth generation produce farmer John Glebocki and Bryan Ensall, who owns a local landscaping business, jointly opened the Orange County Distillery and started selling gin, vodka, bourbon and corn whiskey. The spirits are all distilled in a 100-year old barn from crops grown steps away in Glebocki's Black Dirt fields in Goshen. Glebocki, 36, says he will always be a farmer and the distillery is just a way of adding value to his farm produce. "We are a true 'farm to bottle' craft distillery with a focus on quality, not quantity," says Glebocki. "We grow everything on our farm that we need to produce quality spirits." Twenty of the produce farm's 120 acres are now dedicated to crops for the distillery business.

The two young founders do all the mashing, fermenting, distilling, aging and bottling right in the barn. At present they produce two hundred 375 ml bottles a week and are experimenting with an exotic range of cocktail bitters with flavors from home grown herbs.

The charming, country barn-style tasting room is open every day (12 noon to 5 pm) except Sunday. They produce eight different spirits, though some are often sold out because of their "small batch" emphasis on quality. A range of their products are available for purchase with their farm produce at the Greenmarket in Union Square, New York, on Fridays from 8 am – 6 pm. Theirs are the first and only farm-to-bottle spirits ever sold at that legendary farmers' market in New York City.

Westtown Brew House

Only three years ago Rich Coleman, 37, started his brewing company in neighboring Westtown, on the edge of the Black Dirt, using hops he grows himself. Now he sells a variety of craft beers, including one in which every ingredient is grown right in the Black Dirt. Customers are invited to sit at benches in his garden in the summer, or in a cozy stove-warmed tasting room in the cool months, to try his home brews.

A trained chef, Coleman is also growing lavender, chamomile and lemon verbena for flavoring his beer and hopes to use some of the fruit grown on neighboring farms as well. He sources ingredients locally if possible, including honey for his Three Hives brew, one of his most popular drafts. The tasting room, on a hillside overlooking his hops rows and the Black Dirt fields beyond, has become extremely popular summer and winter. Tasting room hours are 11 am to 6 pm, Saturday and Sunday.

Black Dirt Malt LLC

In an exciting new agricultural venture, in 2014 three farmers planted barley in a collaborative effort to start providing a crop for malting. The barley was so successful in the rich Black Dirt soil that in 2015 dairy farmers Brett Ford and Brian Ford, along with Chip Lain of Pine Island Turf Nursery, a large, established sod farming operation, planted 150 acres of barley.

The three farmers, in collaboration with Black Dirt Distillery, LLC, the distilling arm of Warwick Winery and Distillery nearby, formed Black Dirt Malt, LLC. Chip Lain converted a farm warehouse near his turf nursery office into a professional malting house in compliance with all the regulations controlling premises where food and drink are produced, and a maltatore (malting machine) imported from Italy was installed in August when barley malting began.

Black Dirt Distillery's malt whiskey operation will be the biggest customer. Rich Coleman of Westtown Brew Works will be a customer for his brews and soon Black Dirt Malt hopes to have a tasting room, operated by Coleman's Westtown Brew Works, situated right in the new malt house. "This is the biggest barley farm with its own micro-malt house in New York State," said Chip. "For me, sod farming is still king. But we are very excited about barley."

Mistucky Creek Store

In perfect tune with the trending interest in craft beers and home cellars, the Mistucky Creek Store, providing brewing and wine-making equipment, ingredients and classes for beginners, opened late 2014 in the old Pine Island Firehouse in the heart of the hamlet.

Mistucky Creek was founded by Lloyd Van Duzer of Warwick. A renowned home craft brewer, Van Duzer realized it was difficult to find ingredients in the area so a supply store would fill a growing local need. He sells a range of supplies including starter kits, and makes a point of stocking fresh ingredients. Mistucky Creek also hosts a home brew club that meets monthly.

Kraftify Brewing Company

And in the fall of 2015, the Pine Island Brewing Company had the grand opening of its brew-pub, right next to the Mistucky Creek Store in the old firehouse building. A subset of Kraftify Brewing Company, founded by the entrepreneurial CPA Mike Kraai, the tap house presents customers fresh brewed pints only feet away from where they are created and features all of the brewing equipment on the premises.

Many of the Pine Island Brewing Company brews feature grains and hops grown in the Black Dirt Region. Among the local brews are the Pine Island IPA and Pine Island Scottish Ale. The brewery plans to source locally as much as possible and will return the spent grain, which is good for cattle feed, to local farms.

Your Own Beer Label

"I always dreamed of doing this," says Kraai, who lives with his wife Susan, just 25 miles away in Hawthorne, NJ. "Pine Island, in the Black Dirt region, seemed like the perfect spot." Apart from the six brews on tap under the Pine Island brand, he also offers beer lovers the opportunity to pick a brew and design a personalized label for that beer – a fabulous opportunity for the growing number of beer aficionados to put their own name on a fine beer. Kraai's idea for custom-label brews for gifts or serving at special functions – or just for ego – could prove a winner. The labels can be personally designed on the Kraftify website and the order delivered within a few days.

At the opening of the new Pine Island Brewing Company tap house a couple of old timers shared with young Kraai their memories of the old days in Pine Island when the hamlet was a denizen of drinking establishments. Now, about 40 years later, the Black Dirt region is again getting a name for what and where people drink – but now it's classy tipple, locally brewed or distilled, and almost exclusively produced from crops harvested right in the Black Dirt fields.

Black Dirt Delicious

Food establishments are also among the interesting stories of the uplands. The most famous in foodie circles in the Warwick Valley is the Quaker Creek Country Store on Pulaski Highway. Run by Bobby Matuszewski, who trained at the Culinary Institute of America (CIA), the Quaker Creek store draws customers from a 65 mile radius, including New York City. Instead of a large banner boasting the fact that he was "Featured by Anthony Bourdain", CNN's famous world-travelling food maven, or the subject of an article in *Field and Stream*, or the topic of *"Food Nation"* with Bobby Flay, Matuszewski's business thrives behind a modest storefront. But the word about the gourmet meats and prepared foods is out, as attested by lines often spilling into the parking lot outside Quaker Creek Store.

The soft spoken, sweet natured and energetic Matuszewski trained at the CIA as a *garde manger*, the person who takes care of seasoning, curing, drying, and smoking and in other ways preserving foods. But at heart he is a *wurst macher*, a sausage maker. Beneath the store, Matuszewski has installed a gleaming stainless steel smokehouse. There is a giant metal food processor, with the capacity to mix 200 pounds of meat, and a state of the art machine for filling sausage casings. He makes a range of sausages and specialty foods much loved by the local Polish, German and Italian immigrant communities.

The grandson of a Polish settler who started the Quaker Creek Store, Matuszewski is helped by a number of family members, including his mother, his wife, and his brother. Recently their store became the local outlet for a range of imported European foods.

The Other Harvest

And then there's the other Harvest, a small restaurant right in the heart of the Pine Island hamlet that is a testament to the dreams and possibilities for the newer settlers in the Black Dirt. Though Polish families once ran businesses in the small red brick Harvest building, today it is owned by Jorge Torres, who fled Mexico when he was 17 and with the help of Polish families became what they had become – a successful American.

Torres swam across a river near Tijuana, Mexico, to enter the United States and then travelled across the country, arriving in nearby Goshen with nothing but the clothes he wore. Friends fed and sheltered him for a month until he got a job at the Crystal Inn on the outskirts of Pine Island. "Gus Zygmunt (the owner) gave me a job and over ten years I did just about everything." Torres got a second job at Quaker Creek, working for Barbara Matuszewski, mother of Bobby, who managed the business at the time. "They taught me all about the food business.

"One day I saw that the Country Dream (a diner in nearby Edenville) was looking for help. So I started work there too. So for about four years I was doing three jobs at the same time." During those years he took a trip home to Mexico where he met Galdina Confesor, got married and brought her back to Pine Island. "I decided to raise a family in this great place."

Gus Zygmunt, his boss at the Crystal Inn, bought what was then the Harvest Diner and asked Torres to help manage the eatery. "He said it was a good chance for me to start my own business. I was afraid, but he said he'd help. So I quit Quaker Creek and the Country Dream and just did breakfasts and dinners at the Harvest Diner. Gussie helped me learn how to do the books and told me to save money."

After six years Torres was able to buy the building and the business.

He lived in the apartment attached to the diner for six years, then in 2012 had enough money to buy a house on Kosuga Lane where he and Galdina live with their four boys, now aged 18, 15, 12 and 6, and their new daughter.

When he was working at Crystal Inn, Torres asked Zygmunt to sponsor him for citizenship. "He has helped me all the way. I've now been legal for nine years. Gussie is like my father. I would never have enough money to repay him. He completely trusted me."

He admits some people might not dine at the Harvest simply because he's Mexican. But he shrugs. "I don't dwell on that. There are very nice people in this area. I really thank them for supporting me."

Today, the wall of the Harvest Restaurant is decorated with a mural of Mexican banjo players, and there's a display of Mexican pottery. By the entry door is a prominent notice board that is overwhelmed with local public notices and business cards – evidence of the role this little business plays in the community. "When I took over it was just American breakfast. I added a touch of my own cultural food, and then I added some Italian. So now it's renamed the Harvest Restaurant, serving American, Mexican and Italian - and all three move well." Last year he added beer and wine to the menu.

A few years ago the Torres family won an Appreciation Certificate from the Pine Island Chamber of Commerce for their beautification efforts – the bounty of flowers that every year spill over the brick walls that bound the Harvest parking lot, adding a splash of floral color to the core of the hamlet.

"I have been here 16 years now and have many loyal customers," says Torres. "Now, my kids help in the restaurant and I like that. My wife and I want to show them hard work – and where it can lead them."

J.A.D.S

Right next door to the Harvest Restaurant, at the crossroad in the hamlet, is another colorful community asset – a farm stand where John and Kristie Madura sell vegetables, fruits, garden plants, baked goods, honey, eggs, cheese, home made condiments and frozen grass fed cuts of beef and pork.

The business, known as J.A.D.S. for the initials of their children, Joshua, Alyssa, David and Skyler, is an outlet for some of the produce they grow themselves on their 300-acre farm. What the Maduras don't grow or make themselves, they acquire from local farms.

Apart from Bob and Sally Scheuermann in Little York, J.A.D.S. is the only retail outlet in this agricultural district making a range of fresh, locally grown produce available to the public on a daily basis. Although operating out of a simple shed structure with three canopy walls, the business stays open – rain, snow or cold - from April right through the year until after Christmas.

John Madura, whose father died after being run over by a tractor a few years ago, grows a wide range of vegetables and herbs in his Black Dirt fields beside the Wallkill River. He also has high tunnels enabling him to produce flowers, herbs and vegetables throughout the year, and he has a room dedicated to growing eight varieties of mushrooms, which have become one of his specialties.

Every morning Madura gets up at 4.30, when foxes and deer are still lurking in the dark, to supervise the loading of his trucks bound for the farmer's markets he serves in the New York boroughs and Ossining, upstate NY.

His wife Kristie manages the J.A.D.S. farm stand and has become renowned for the witticisms she puts on the roadside sign where she announces the fresh produce of the day. Among them….

"Gardening is better than therapy, and you get tomatoes"
"We are so happy it's spring, we wet our plants"
"We ain't sassy, but we sure are corny"
"Create a Fabulous Fall look with Freakishly low prices"

Apart from produce, the Madura's sell topsoil, Christmas wreaths and trees, spring flowers and herbs. They also offer a CSA (Community Supported Agriculture) contract whereby customers pay at the start of the season for the coming years' produce as it ripens.

Several times during the weather catastrophes of recent years the J.A.D.S. stand was destroyed by wind or collapsed under the weight of snow – and the community held its breath. Will they be back? Every time the couple restored the structure, and restocked the fridges and tables with produce. But now the J.A.D.S. farm stand is a solid structure with a corrugated iron roof, painted red and white for the colors of the Polish flag. It's a structure that proudly withstood the record snow that fell in the Black Dirt in the winter of 2014-2015, and opened, with flowers and vegetables fresh from the Madura's high-tunnels, on April 1.

Black Dirt Proud

Over the years, "Black Dirt" has become a proud brand name – the word "dirt" associated not with "dirty" but with a fabulously fertile soil. For more than 25 years local businesses have branded themselves "Black Dirt" – a hair salon, a printing operation, a dance school, and even a food business: Cheryl Rogowski chose Black Dirt Gourmet as the name for the catering operation she founded in her barn with the cash she got as part of her McArthur Award in 2004. As mentioned earlier, through Black Dirt Gourmet she has sold a wide range of foods made from the produce of the region and created a field-to-fork catering business, something she hopes to do again when her current financial woes are resolved.

Every summer since 2009 the Pine Island Chamber of Commerce has organized the biggest foodie event in the region, the renowned Black Dirt Feast. The six-course dinner, served Tuscan style at long tables on the great lawn at Scheuermann Farms and Greenhouses, is a celebration of the locally grown food and the chefs of the region who use it in their restaurants. The brainchild of the creative Pine Island entrepreneurs Peter and Sondra Hall, it is now organized by John Redman of the Union Square Group and has been sold out every year since inception. Proceeds fund agricultural or culinary college education scholarships.

The Pine Island Chamber of Commerce puts on two other events celebrating the produce of the region in the valley every year. The Raw Onion Eating Contest is held late summer – usually in conjunction with the Jimmy Sturr Onion Festival in the pavilion at the Polish Legion Post 19 late summer. And Pumpkin Fest, held every Columbus Day in the Pine Island Park, is a colorful and fun-filled tribute to the fall crop, attended by hundreds of children.

Not all the activity is around the crossroads. Tucked in the woods and old farmhouses that scatter the region are distinguished and award winning artists and photographers. Jonathan Talbot in Amity is a world-renowned collage artist, his works in collections in the U.S. and around the world. The exquisite glass art works of Gary Genetti are in collections in the Smithsonian Museum. Laura Breitman's collage pictures from almost imperceptible dots of fabric and paper are in galleries and museums throughout the United States, including the Museum of Arts and Design in New York. And in the woods near the New Jersey border lives Barbara Lanza, the children's book illustrator, designer and a nationwide expert on how to paint fairies, which may, or may not, abound in the Black Dirt valley. And there are many more.

Some of the blocky, low warehouses from onion farming's heyday now house new enterprises. John Redman moved his Union Square Group from Manhattan to a warehouse off Mission Land Road. Here Redman makes sets for everything from Broadway shows and music concerts to corporate promotions and shopping mall extravaganzas across the country.

But many warehouses that once stored onions or other produce are now empty. Andy Field, the property developer who owns some large buildings in Pine Island, says most of the warehouses are now in disrepair. Regulations governing repair or restoration of these old farm buildings are so strict that bringing them up to code is prohibitively expensive, he says. "Its cheaper to build something new. That's why many of the warehouses in Pine Island are rotting.

However, Field is a visionary who believes that Pine Island, being situated in the heart of the Black Dirt valley, is strategically very well located. He sees it as a hub, a hamlet filled with agricultural and food based retailers, especially on the commercially pivotal site at the crossroads that was the home of the famous Jolly Onion Inn. It's a property he owns with Will Brown, owner of nearby Lowland Farm, home to grass fed beef, sheep, and pigs.

The two say they are confident that as the economy improves, investors will come to the Jolly Onion with an idea for a locavore restaurant, or maybe a store selling locally grown foods. Evidence of his confidence is the fact he has been investing in the hamlet for many years. "In my view," says Field, "The Black Dirt region, and Pine Island at its core, is the future, the productive heart of the Warwick valley."

Black Dirt Booze Links

Orange County Distillery. (http://orangecountydistillery.com)
Westtown Brew House. (www.Westtownbrewworks.com)
Warwick Valley Winery. (http://www.wvwinery.com)
Mistucky Creek Store (www.Mistuckycreek.com)
Pine Island Brewing/Kraftify Brewing Company. (www.Kraftifybrewing.com)
Black Dirt Malt. LLC. https://www.facebook.com/blackdirtmalt

CHAPTER 12: CBD IN THE BLACK DIRT

When the Farm Bill passed in December 2018 legalizing growth of hemp for cannabidiol – the "wellness" oil extract known as CBD - there was an explosion of interest among farmers in the Black Dirt region.

There are 1,700 acres in New York State already under hemp. Almost 20 Black Dirt farmers have taken on the high cost, high risk and potentially highly profitable crop. And more are expected to start growing hemp for CBD.

So prolific are the hemp plants along Pulaski Highway, in the heart of the Black Dirt, that this harvest season - when the air is usually filled with the pungent aroma of onions- the smell of marijuana (some consider it the smell of skunk) was everywhere.

The boom in CBD hemp farming "is like the wild west," says Maire Ullrich, the Cornell Extension Office agriculture leader, and the head of their cannabis team. Some of the biggest names in Black Dirt agriculture – Minkus, Dagele, Kokot, Ford, Rogowski, Pawelski, Madura - are now grow-ing some hemp for CBD. It's possible to gross $40,000 - $60,000 an acre – unheard of in conventional produce farming.

Cannabidiol is not marijuana and crops are inspected before harvesting to ensure that CBD hemp plants do not contain more than 0.3% of tetrahydrocannabinol (THC), the ingredient that creates a "high". CBD, which is extracted from the buds, is used for depression, sleeplessness, anxiety, Parkinson's Disease, MLS, Lou Gehrig's disease, arthritis pain and more.

Within months of the Farm Bill's passage Brian Ford, the oldest brother in the largest dairy farming family in the region, planted 35,000 plants on 25 acres in the heart of the Black Dirt region. Each plant produces about a pound of CBD.

Marshall Swartwood, a successful investment banker from nearby Westtown, joint ventured with Ford in the hemp growing enterprise. A newcomer to farming at age 84, Swartwood said that hemp transplantings cost about $2 or $3 each – far more than most crops. Overall operating costs run to about $7,000 an acre. However, farmers can earn 10 times as much from hemp as from regular produce.

Swartwood showed me their hemp plants, with their decorative, almost fern-like leaves, planted three feet apart along plastic strips that prohibit weed growth. Below the plants are irrigation lines. He uses strictly organic pesticide and herbicide practices.

He said that the hemp plants thrive in the Black Dirt, with its 55% organic matter – compared with 5% in regular soil. As a result, the CBD content in the rich black soil is as high as 15%, compared with 7-9% in ordinary soil.

A problem is that hemp farming is labor intensive – 8 to 10 workers are needed for an 8-hour day when planting is done by hand, he said. Only female plants produce CBD, so male or pollinated plants must be fastidiously removed. After about three months the plants stand three to four feet high and must also be harvested by hand - mechanization for CBD hemp is still scarce.

Ford created the first processing plant in the Black Dirt region, and formed two limited liability companies, Black Dirt Canna, and Black Dirt CBD, to produce CBD products – all at a cost of about $1 million. They dry the plants, separate the CBD hemp buds to extract the oil, and using the extracted oil, they produce a lotion which sells for $35, and droplet bottles of strawberry and chocolate flavored tinctures, selling for $75 each.

The CEO of Black Dirt Canna and Black Dirt CBD, Michael White, said the market was certain to grow. He knew of a high-end restaurant chef looking into adding CBD to his food. Customers would pay more, but feel better. And pain management doctors at nearby Crystal Run Health Centre were looking into using CBD oil for patient treatment.

However, there is some caution among farmers. Chip Lain, a successful sod farmer who teamed up with Brian Ford to produce malted barley for the craft brew industry, said he would wait and see how the hemp business did before getting involved. Chris Pawelski, whose partner and brother, Brian Pawelski, is growing CBD hemp, said for him it was too risky, expensive and had no guaranteed market. He was staying with onions for the time being.

Growers and processors must each obtain a license from New York state. There are many more growers than processors and New York has stopped giving licenses for processing. Maire Ullrich at the CCE said the problem for growers to find processors has already limited the potential profits for CBD hemp growers.

As yet there are limited regulations and distribution controls and no CBD hemp crop insurance. Scientific research into the crop is taking place at every level and state and federal strict regulations, like those effecting tobacco and alcohol, are expected to soon impact the CBD hemp business.

Towards the end of the 2019 harvesting season Maire Ullrich added that average costs were running higher, at $10-20K per acre, and the gross profit for CBD had dropped to more like $25-$30K an acre.

None of that, said Ullrich, had diminished interest. The number of farmers keen to start planting CBD hemp in the Black Dirt continued to grow. Brian Ford and Michael White at Black Dirt Canna said they planned to expand their start-up operation from 25 acres to 50 acres next season.

Across the US more than 200,000 acres of hemp were licensed to be planted in the U.S. this year (2019), up from roughly 25,000 two years ago. According to researchers quoted in Bloomberg Business Week, the market for CBD in the U.S. alone could be worth about 24 billion dollars by 2023.

And here the Black Dirt, the fabulously fertile soil so long associated with onions and "field to fork" fresh produce, might also soon become a mega-million dollar source for CBD hemp. ■

CHAPTER 13: OTHER CHANGES COME TO THE BLACK DIRT VALLEY

Labor

Some of the most significant recent changes affect farm labor. The growing shortage of immigrant workers was dramatically exacerbated after 2016 when President Donald Trump came into office (with the vote of most Black Dirt farmers) with a policy that severely threatened undocumented immigrants - the status of most farm workers in the region. Some long loyal workers fled, and the number of new-comers, willing to risk confrontations with ICE and deportation, dropped. The percentage of farmers now using the complicated, burdensome H-2A visa for farm workers has grown. The shortage continues, exacerbated by the fact that farming hemp for CBD is labor-intensive.

The situation is worsened by the fact that the existing agricultural farm worker population working in the Black Dirt region and throughout the state is getting older. The physically challenging work is being done by men and women whose average age is 38. The switch to crops that can be maintained and harvested by machines slowly grows.

The laws affecting farm workers in New York State were dramatically changed in 2019 by the new Farmworkers Fair Labor Practices Act, introduced after Democrats took over the NY senate – thus controlling both houses of the state legislature. The biggest effect came from the controversial introduction of overtime pay after 60 hours of work in a week. There were some workers who opposed overtime pay because they preferred long work hours during growing seasons since they don't have agricultural work when the season is over. They knew enforced overtime pay would lead to a cut in their working hours. Meantime, the US Department of Agriculture is working on simplifying the H-2A visa and cutting the paperwork to help reduce the farm labor shortage, a problem across the country.

Farms and Farmers

The average age of farmers in the US continues to rise. However, in the Black Dirt region second generation farmers in their twenties and thirties are thriving. Maire Ullrich, Agricultural Leader at the Cornell Extension Office, reports that there is also a growth of new farmers under 40 years old, many of whom have no farming experience at all. The number of farmers who are not of the region's traditional Polish and German origins has also grown: Hispanic (about eight farms) and Asian (about four farms).

Onions are still the dominant crop but prices farmers receive are historically and inexplicably low, even though market prices have risen. Following an appeal by onion farmer Chris Pawelski, Senator Kirsten Gillibrand (D. NY) has asked the Secretary of Agriculture to investigate the pricing structure of the fresh produce industry. Pawelski believes the culprits are chain stores which dictate prices to packers.

Federal data show that in New York State the number of farms declined by 6% between 2012 and 2017, and about 11,000 acres of produce went out of production. The low profits on onions and other produce are considered a reason why many Black Dirt farmers are testing hemp as a crop.

President Donald Trump's policy on Chinese tariffs has seriously hurt the soybean growers, but losses have been offset somewhat by Federal payouts. Some older farmers are giving up land for solar power production, which brings payments that continue well into their old age. The small number of "Certified Organic" farms in the weed-loving black dirt has diminished further, but the wave toward "Certified Naturally Grown," using organic practices, continues to grow across all crops grown in Black Dirt farmlands.

The best known "USDA Certified Organic" are the super-healthy wheatgrass and microgreens raised by Harley Matsil and his family. Their Perfect Foods indoor operation on Pulaski Highway is now one of the largest suppliers of wheatgrass in the United States, and provides as much as 90% of the superfood consumed in New York City.

Weather and Water

After several years of work, the flood mitigation benches have been completed by the Orange County Soil and Water Conservation District along a section of the Wallkill River's bank. The benches were an excavation about 50 feet wide to lower both river banks to allow more efficient flow of the water in times of flooding. John Ruszkiewicz, 83, an active onion farmer and the region's historian, reports that those farming near the river region express satisfaction with the results – there have been no floods. However, there has not in recent years been a catastrophic downpour like those that devastated the black dirt farmland in years past – most recently in 2011. A budget of $400,000 is still available for flood control measures – possibly more benches. But many farmers still push for more powerful measures to curb flooding from the severe downpour that will come one day.

Agritourism Uptick

The recent growth of breweries, cideries, distilleries and wineries in the Black Dirt area continues, contributing to a huge increase in agritourism. Maire Ullrich of the Cornell Extension Office reports that city folk are now coming to the region in busloads.

A major, much welcomed contribution to the tourism uptick is the 2018 reopening of The Jolly Onion, the famous restaurant at the heart of Pine Island, which was closed in 2008. Warwick resident Tom Mastrantoni, owner of the Italian deli Roccoroma in Goshen, manages the new Jolly Onion Team which includes Chef Armand Vanderstigchel, author of Adirondack Cuisine, Wings Across America, and Adirondack Cookbook. Mastrantoni said he plans to focus on local food, work with farmers, keep the downstairs rooms as catering/event space and maintain the Jolly as a hub for the community.

Opposite the Jolly Onion, on land they once rented out to JADS farm market (long departed Pine Island), the Porter family are building another micro-brewery. And further down Glenwood Road, Don Oriolo, a wealthy artist and musician, has created Blue Arrow Farm, a beautifully restored horse farm, art gallery and entertainment center for concerts, weddings and, possibly one day a microbrewery. Oriolo, whose father created the Felix the Cat franchise, bought the farm in 2017 to create a "destination" – adding to the cultural draw of the Black Dirt region.

A growing tourist mecca in the Black Dirt is the Warwick Valley Winery, drawing ever larger crowds to wine, cider and spirits tastings and music concerts. The former head chef at the winery, John Castrovillari, has now teamed up with his partner, Lauren Grace, to form Pitchfork Barbecue and Biscuits, a wood-fired mobile smoker which they park near the charming Pine Island Park and serve craft BBQ and from-scratch-made buttermilk biscuits on Thursday through Sunday.

These are just some of the additions to the appeal of the Black Dirt region. Farmer Leonard DeBuck, President of the Pine Island Chamber of Commerce, says that the proximity to New York City draws large crowds yearning for "a day in the country." Sometimes the "agritainment" has led to complaints and the Town of Warwick is now looking into applying regulations that will limit the "agrivation" from agritourism.

But overall, in terms of the benefits agritourism brings to the Black Dirt Valley, notes DeBuck, "the future looks good." ■

America's Favorite Sweet Onion. Vidalia Onion Committee. Vidaliaonion.org. n.d. Web. (June, 2014)

American Farmland Trust: *"No Farms. No Food."* n.d. Website. farmland.org/no-farms-no-food. 2015. (Oct, 2015.)

Anon. *The History of the Black Dirt Region*. Pine Island NY Chamber of Commerce. Web. Retrieved Feb, 2014. (Oct, 2015)

Anon. "Black Market for Black Soil." *Kyiv Post*, Nov. 9, 2011.

Anon. "St Peter's Lutheran Church to Mark 65th Anniversary." (History of Volga Germans) *The Warwick Advertiser*. July 1965. (Transcription by Terry Hann, 2010) (Oct, 2015)

Anon. "Warwick Valley Farm Aid Raises $100,000." *Warwick Chamber of Commerce Community News*. Oct 14, 2011. Web. Warwickcc.org (Oct, 2015)

Bittman Mark. "Stop Making Us Guinea Pigs." *New York Times*. (Opinion Pages.) March 25, 2015.

Bittman, Mark. "Celebrate the Farmer!" *New York Times*. Opinionator Blog. Aug 21, 2012. Web. Opinionator.blogs.nytimes.com (Oct 20, 20150

Brenner, Leslie. *American Appetite: The Coming of Age of a National Cuisine.* (New York.) William Morrow. (1999)

Brill, Peter. *A History of the Middletown and New Jersey Railroad, LLC, and Predecessors.* Part I: The Middletown, Unionville & Water Gap (MU&WG). For Middletown & New Jersey Railway Historical Society. n.d. Web. mnjrhs.org (Oct, 2015)

Bronars, Stephen G. *A Vanishing Breed: How the Decline in U.S. Farm Laborers Over the past Decade has Hurt the U.S. Economy and Slowed Production on American Farms.* Prepared for Partnership for a New American Economy. July 2015. Web. Renewoureconomy.com (Oct, 2015)

Campaign For Fair Food. *Coalition of Immokalee Food Workers*. n.d. Web. ciw-on-line.org (Dec 12, 2014.)

Certification/Recertification Packet For New Private Pesticide Applicators. (Pesticide Safety Education Program. Cornell University Cooperative Extension. 2013. Web. Psep.cce.cornell.edu. (Oct, 2015.)

Chase, Spencer. "Vilsack says immigration reform critical for future of food supply." *Agri-Pulse*. Dec 4, 2014. Web. Agri-Pulse.comHH22-A Visas:

"Chernozem." *Britannica.com.* 2015. Web.

"Copper (11) Sulfate. Human Health Effects." *Toxicology Data Network.* n.d. Web.http://toxnet.nlm.nih.gov/ (Oct, 2015)

D'Attolico, "Organic Farm: How to Recognize a Fresh String Bean." Cravings Productions. n.d. Video. vimeo.com. (Oct, 2015)

Davenport, Coral. "Obama Announces New Rule Limiting Water Pollution." *New York Times.*   May 27, 2015. (July, 2015.)

DerVartanian, Adrienne. "Migration Policy Institute Briefing on Farm Labor." FarmworkerJustice.org. Sept 25, 2015. Blog. (Oct 19,2015)

DeSanto, John. "How the Drowned Lands became the Black Dirt." *Times Herald-Record.* Jan 15, 2015. (Oct, 2015)

"Documenting the Agricultural Records of the Black Dirt Region." (DeBuck Sod Farms.) *Middletown Thrall Library.* 1997-98. Thrall.org. Web. (Feb, 2014)

Easley, Hema. "A farmer's dream come true: land to farm." *Times Herald-Record.* Nov. 17, 2014. Web. Recordonline.com. (Oct 3, 2015.)

Edelstein, Michael R. "Irene, Irene, best reason for restoring wetlands I've ever seen." In My View, September, 2011 Orange Environment. 2011. Web. orangeenvironment.org (Oct 20, 2015)

El-Ghobashy, Tamir. "New York's Orange County Left Crippled by Floods." *Wall Street Journal.* Aug 29, 2011. Blog. (Oct 15, 2015)

"Environmental Impact Quotient." *New York State Integrated Pest Management Program.* Cornell University. n.d.Web. nysipm.cornell.edu (Oct, 2015)

Environmental Working Group. "2012 Farm Subsidy Database." 2013.   Web. Farm.EWG.org. (Oct, 2015)

Farm to Institution, NYS. "Linking Farmers to Institutional Markets in New York." *American Farmland Trust.* 2015. Website. Farmland.org. (Oct, 2015)

Fodaro, Lisa W. "Fickle Tastes and Prices Idle Onion Farmers." *New York Times* May 7, 1990. Print.

Foderaro, Lisa. "New York Trash Haulers Charged With Bribery and Payoffs to Mob." *New York Times.* Oct 9, 1991. Print.

Food & Drug Administration. "Strengthening Oversight of Food Imports." *Consumer Health Information.* July 30, 2013. Web. FDA.Gov/consumer (Oct , 2015)

Food & Water Watch. *Grocery Goliaths: How Food Monopolies Impact Consumers.* Dec 2013. Web. Foodandwaterwatch.org (Feb 20, 2015)

Glynwood Center. *The State of Agriculture in the Hudson Valley.* (2005, updated 2007, 2010). Print and online. Glynwood.org. (Oct, 2015)

Gramley, Richard Michael. "The ASAA Mastodon...Orange County, NY." n.d. Paper for *American Society for Amateur Archaeology.* The Amateur Archeologist Online. Web. (Oct. 2015)

Groome, Debra J. "Nutient Rich Muck Makes Perfect Soil..." *The Post Standard.* (Syracuse) July 06, 2009. (Oct, 2015)

Haumann, Barbara. "Consumer-driven U.S. organic market surpasses $31 billion in 2011." *Organic Trade Association* Press Release, 2012. Web. Organicnewsroom.com (Oct, 2015)

Hepker, Caroline. "Food waste reduction could help feed world's starving." (Re; Chris Pawelski.) *BBC World Business Report.* July 3 2014, Web. BBC.Com

Hoppe, Robert. "Profit Margin Increases With Farm Size." *United States. Department of Agriculture.* Economic Research Service. n.d. Web. ERS.USDA.Gov. (Feb 20, 2015)

Hull, Richard W. *People of the Valleys Revisited. History of Warwick, New York, 1700-2005.* Richard W. Hull @2005.

Isaac, Rael Jean. *Harvest of Injustice: Legal Services vs. The Farmer,* (1996), National Legal and Policy Center, Falls Church, VA. (2014)

Isseks, Fred. *Choke Point on the Cheechunk.* Published Dec 19, 2014. (Tour organized by the Hudson River Environmental Society, fall of 2013.) Video. Youtube.com (Oct 18, 2015)

Isseks, Fred. *The Wallkill River, the Cheechunk Canal, and the Orange County Landfill: a brief history and a reflection.* Blog and Website. Dec 11, 2014. (Feb 20, 2015.)

Karst, Tom. "E-Verify legislation draws industry fire." *The Packer.* March 05, 2015. Print and Web. Thepacker.com. (Oct 16.2015)

King, Matt. "11,000-year-old Moose Elk Found." *Times-Herald Record* (Middletown, NY). Nov. 8, 2007. Print. (Oct, 2015)

Kopicki, Allison. "Strong Support for Labeling Modified Foods." *New York Times*, July 27, 2013. Print. (Oct 2015)

Lambert, Emily. *The Futures: The Rise of the Speculator and the Origins of the World's Biggest Markets.* New York: Basic Books Dec 28, 2010 (ebook at Bookchums.com).

Lee, Matt and Ted. "A Glacial Secret Told by Onions,." *New York Times*. Oct 24, 2007. Print. (Oct, 2015)

Levy, Sharon. "Mammoth Mystery". OnEarth.org. Winter 2006. Web. (Oct, 2015)

Lomborg, Bjorn. *The Skeptical Environmentalist.* Cambridge. UK. Cambridge University Press,); 1st edition (September 10, 2001)

Maurer, Daniel. "Meet the Star-mer." (Alex Paffenroth) *New York Magazine.* Aug 3, 2008. Web. NYmag.com.(Oct 15 2013)

McArdle, Megan. "Georgia's Harsh Immigration Law Costs Millions in Unharvested Crops." *The Atlantic,* June 21, 2011. Print (Feb 20, 2015.)

McCandless, Linda. "Rogowski wins a MacArthur 'Genius' Award." *Cornell Chronicle.* Nov 11, 2004

McGee, Harold. *On Food and Cooking: The Science and Lore of the Kitchen.* New York: Scribner, 1984 & 2004.

McKinley, Jesse. "Picking New York State's Soil? Not so Fast." *New York Times.* March 27, 2013. (Oct, 2015)

Moskin, Julia. "Hold the Regret? Fast Food Seeks a Virtuous Side." *New York Times.* July 25, 2015.

Moskin, Julia. "Women Find Their Place in the Field." *New York Times* June 1, 2005

Murrow, Edward R. "Harvest of Shame." *CBS News.* 1960. YouTube uploaded Nov 24, 2010.YouTube.com. (Oct, 2015)

"National Agricultural Workers Survey." *U.S. Dept of Labor: Employment and Training Administration.* Mar 27, 2004, Updated Jan 11, 2010. doleta.gov (Oct 20, 2015.)

"New York Bold." New York Bold. n.d. web. (Jan, 2014)

Northeast Beginning Farmers Project. Website. Cornell University. 2015. nebeginningfarmers.org (Oct, 2015) University of Nebraska, Lincoln. "Case Study Report."

Ojito, Mirta. "At a Farm Market, an Absence Is Noted." (Vincent D'Attolico.) *New York Times*. Sept 14, 1997. (Sept. 2013)

"Onion Health Research." *National Onion Association*. Onions.USA.org. n.d. Web. (Jan, 2014.)

"Onions are Beneficial to our Health." *Vegetarianism and Vegetarian Nutrition*. Andrews University, MI. Vegetarian-nutritian.com. Web n.d. (Jan 2014.)

Orange County Land Trust. *Hudson Valley Farmlink Network* n.d. Website. OCLT.org. (Oct, 2015)

Orange County, NY. Farm Viability in Urbanizing Areas. 2008. With Cornell Cooperative Extension. Univ. Nebraska. Web. (March, 2014.

Pauly, Alexandra. *The Best Weekend Getaways In America*," Jan, 2014. stylecaster.com. Web. (Oct, 2015)

Pawelski, Chris. *1955 flood and farming in the black dirt of Orange County in 1950s*. Youtube.com. youtube.com/watch?v=TjK16lwupGg . (March 27, 2014.)

Pawelski, Chris. *Rural and Migrant Ministry Executive Director Richard Witt tells a whopper*. YouTube. Uploaded May 29, 2009.
https://www.youtube.com/watch?v=JMWTHBkUuHk

Pawelski, Chris. "The backstory behind my $150,000 50lb bag of onions on eBay." *Muckville.com*. Jan 13, 2014. Blog. (Jan, 2014)

Pawelski, Chris. "Advocating for America's Specialty Crop Family Farms". *Farmroot.org*. n.d. (Oct, 2015)

Revken, Andrew. "On Green Dread and Agricultural Technology." *New York Times*, July 22, 2011. Print.

Richards, Linda. "Onions Can Help Prevent Inflammation." *Arthritis Foundation*. Web. Arthritis.org. n.d. (May, 2014.)

Rivers, Tom. *Farm Hands: Hard Work and Hard Lessons from Western New York Fields*. Tom Rivers, 2010. (July 6, 2013.)

Sainath, P. "Knowing your onions in New York." *The Hindu*. Dec 3, 2012

Serrao, John. "Purple Tomatoes Go GMO to Cure Cancer." *Nutrition Wonderland*. Nov 26, 2008. Web. Nutritionwonderland.com (Oct, 2015)

Severson, Kim. "Vidalia Onions: A Crop With an Image to Uphold." *New York Times*. April 7, 2014. Print. (Oct, 2015)

Smallwood, Karl. "Vincent Kosuga and His Onions." *Today I Found Out*. Apr 23, 2014. Blog. (Oct, 2015)

Smallwood, Karl. "The Most Evil Businessman in History was an Onion Farmer." *Fact Fiend*. Aug 5, 2013. Blog. (Oct, 2015)

Smith, Bren. "Don't Let Your Children Grow up to be Farmers." *New York Times*. Aug 9, 2014. Print. (Oct, 2015)

Smith, Edward. *The Vegetable Gardener's Bible*. (MA, USA.) Storey Publishing, 2009. (Jan, 2014)

Snell, James P. *Drowned Lands of the Wallkill, Including the Beaver and Muskrat War,* As recorded in History of Sussex and Warren Co., 1881 (Transcribed by Joe Bartolotta, Feb, 2004). Albertwisnerlibrary.org. Web. (Oct. 2015)

Souza, Bianca. "Pine Island 'Onion King' passes away at 86." *Times Herald-Record*. Jan 21, 2001. (Feb 2014)

Sullivan, John. "Historic' floods engulf mid-Hudson." *Times Herald-Record*. Aug 29, 2011. Print. (Oct, 2015)

Sunken, Alyssa. "Farmers push government for storm aid." *Times-Herald Record,* Sept 6, 2011. Web. Recordonline.com. (Sept 8, 2011.)

Take Our Jobs."United Farm Workers." 2010. Web. *UFW.Org*. (Feb, 2013)

Texas A&M University. "Genetically Modified Carrots Provide Easy To Absorb Calcium." *ScienceDaily*. ScienceDaily, 16 January 2008. Sciencedaily.com (Oct, 2015)

U.S. Department of Agriculture Economic Research Service. *Farm Labor*. n.d. ers.usda.gov/topics/farm-economy/farm-labor.aspx (Oct, 2015)

U.S. Fish and Wildlife Service. *Indiana Bat (Myotis sodalis)*. n.d. Web. FWS.Gov.(Oct , 2015)

U.S. Department of Labor Employment and Training Admin. *National Agricultural Workers Survey*. Ch. 3. n.d. Web. (Oct.2015)

Van Meter, Jonathan. "In Hillary's Footsteps: Kirsten Gillibrand." *Vogue*. Oct 19, 2010. Print. (Oct, 2015)

Von Mogel, Karl Haro. "UK must lead the World in GM crops." *Biology Fortified.* June 20, 2013. Web. Biofortified.com. (Sept, 2015.)

Walsh, James. "City Greenmarkets healthy for mid-Hudson farmers." (Alex Paffenroth) *Times Herald-Record.* Sep. 22, 2013. Web. Recordonline.com. (Oct, 2013.)

Walsh, James. "Medical Pot Companies Seek Foothold. " *Times Herald-Record* May 26, 2015. Print.

INTERVIEWS

(In Person, Online and by Phone.)

Bracco, Tony. Owner/Grower, Bracco Farm (2014)

Brieger, Katherine. Executive, HudsonRiver Health Care (2014)

Coleman, Rich. Owner, Westtown Brew House, (2014)

Dagele, Frank. Managing Partner Farmer, Dagele Bros. (2013, 2014)

DeBuck, Gregory. Manager, DeBuck Sod Farms, (2013, 2014)

deLeon, Hortensia. Field worker and packer. (2014)

Edelstein, Michael. President, Orange Environment. (2015)

Fernandez, Mario. The Farmworkers Center ("Alamo.") (2013)

Field, Andy. Andrew Field Real Estate, 2012, (July 2013,)

Glebocki, John. Partner, Orange County Distillery, Grower, Glebocki Farms (2015)

Grajewski, Stash. Director, Farm Workers Community Centre – "Alamo." (2013, 2015)

Gurda, Andrew. Owner, A Gurda Produce. (2014)

Kelsey Lain. Farm Office Manager, Pineturf Nursery (2013, 2014)

Gurda, Michelle. A Gurda Farms, (2013)

Gurda, Stanley. Ret. Grower Gurda Farms. (2015)

Hamburger, Jane. Retired Principal, Pine Island Elementary School (2014)

Hull, Richard W. Warwick Historian, (2014, 2015)

Kidde, Jeremy. Partner, Warwick Valley Winery and Distillery, (2015)

Kocot, Alex. Grower/Owner, Harvest Queen Farm. (2015)

Kosuga, Polly. (1915-2009) Philanthropist, Widow of Vincent Kosuga, (2004)

Kowall, Russell. Grower/Owner Kowall Farms, Warwick Town Councilman (2013)

Lain, Chip. Owner, Pine Turf Nursery, Black Dirt Malt, LLC, (2014, 2015)

Lain, Charlie, Ret. Owner Pine Turf Nursery. (2014)

Luna, Gerardo. Migrant Farm Field worker. (2014)

Madura, Kristie, Manager, JADS Farm Market, (2015)

Madura, John David. Grower Owner, Madura Farms, (2012)

Matuszewski, Bobby. Owner, Quaker Creek Store, (2014, 2015)

Mendoza, Juan. Mexican Farm Worker. (2013)

Minkus, Tom. Minkus Family Farm, (2013)

Morgiewicz, Joe. Partner-owner, Morgiewicz Farms, (2014,2015)

Mosher, Daryl. Asst Prof of Culinary Arts, Culinary Institute of America (2014)

Paffenroth, Alex. Owner, Paffenroth Gardens. (2013, 2014)

Pahucki, Tom, Former Orange County Legislator, Associate Broker; Keller Williams Realty (2013)

Pawelski, Grace. Pawelski Farms (2013)

Rawal, Sanjay. Movie Director. "Food Chains." (2013)

Rogowski, Cheryl. Owner, W. Rogowski Farms, Black Dirt Gourmet. (2013, 204, 2015)

Ruszkiewicz, Paul, President, Orange County Vegetable Growers Association, Orange County Legislator. (2014, 2015)

Scheuermann, Sally and Bob. Owners, Scheuermann Farms and Greenhouses. (2013.)

Schultz, Stanley (1919-2012), Founder, Pine Island Chamber of Commerce. (2009)

Sobiech, Brennan. Grower, Brennan E Sobiech Farms, LLC (2013)

Sobiech, Tom. Pipeline Industry Expert. (2014, 2015)

Sumner, Kevin. Orange County Soil & Water District (2013, 2015)

Sweeton, Michael. Warwick Town Supervisor (2014)

Talbot, Marsha. Better Homes/Rand Realty, Warwick (2014)

Torres, Jorge. Owner-manager, Harvest Restaurant, (2013, 2015)

Valle, Lidia. Farm worker. (2014)

Wagner, Pam. Fran Liston. Sisters of the Divine Compassion, Mustard Seed Ministry, (2015)

Zygmunt, Gus. Owner, Crystal Inn, (2015)

IMAGES

Cover photo: *Pine Island Black Dirt* by Robert Breese/breesepix. Used with permission.

Page ii: Google Earth and Google Maps.

Page viii: Pine Island Map by Ken Pinkham, ERS Consultants. Used with permission

Chapter 1: Aerial of Black Dirt Region by John Stage. Used with permission.

Chapter 2: Polish Dancers, by John Stage. Used with permission.

Chapter 3: Onion Capital of the World, Pine Island Chamber of Commerce.

Chapter 4: Vince Kosuga (Kosuga family) and Chicago Mercantile Exchange photo.

Chapter 5: Rock Stars illustration from FreePik.com, adapted by Peter Lyons Hall.

Chapter 6: *Drowned Lands* by Robert Breese/breesepix. Used with permission.

Chapter 7: *Spring Planting Farmhands* by John Stage. Used with permission.

Chapter 8: *Pesticides* Onion thrips, Diane Alston, Utah State University, Bugwood.org

Chapter 9: *Pine Island Roadside Farm Stand*, by John Stage. Used with permission.

Chapter 10: *Farm Truck Pumpkins*, Shutterstock. Used with permission.

Chapter 11: *Post Script*, Black Dirt Feast, courtesy of Jia Han Dong, 500px.com/jiahandong

Chapter 12: Hemp plant, courtesy of Pixabay.com